The GOP  for 2016

By Xiaofeng "Frank" Li, Ph.D.

To: Dean Ciluffo

From: Frank Li

12/13/2013

Text copyright © 2013 Frank Li
All Rights Reserved

"*Democracy is the road to socialism.*"
--- Karl Marx

"*Democracy is when the indigent, and not the men of property, are the rulers.*"
--- Aristotle, 350BC

Book Reviews

"This is an important book for all Americans to read. Frank Li has succeeded in condensing political strategy into a very readable presentation. His prescription for a philosophical rebirth of the Republican Party is straightforward: Move toward a majority of the populace on social issues, stay solidly on a capitalist footing, encourage legal immigration and put sound monetary and fiscal practices in place. He is very critical of policies of the Democratic Party and also of some Republicans. This will be a difficult book for some politicians to read but many citizens who do read it will start looking for office seekers who have a clear vision like the one Dr. Li has espoused."

--- **John Lounsbury**, Ph.D., Managing Editor, Global Economic Intersection (NC)

"In his last book ('Saving America, Chinese Style'), Frank Li explained why the U.S. is 'deeply in trouble.' In this new book, he tries to count on the GOP to lead the U.S. out of the trouble. As an independent, Frank is highly critical of the Democratic Party, as well as some Republicans. He defines and explains both democratic imperialism and democratic socialism very well in this book, and blames both of them for America's 'steep decline.' Frank ponders where we will now find leaders like Lincoln, Truman, Nixon, and Reagan. His cross-cultural analysis challenges us to think differently. His solutions are controversial but are fresh and cross party lines. Overall, this is definitely a book worth reading."

--- **Brad Lewis**, Ph.D., Professor of Economics, Union College (Schenectady, NY)

"Again, Dr. Li has produced a fantastic book as great as his first one. Again, not only did I enjoy reading it, I also learned a great deal from it. Dr. Li expressed a lot of facts, summations, interpretations, and very gutsy predictions with lots of original ideas and references, in plain English. The issues facing our country are real and very scary. I wish more Americans will become more informed by reading this book."

--- **Gary Wetzel**, COO/CFO, Wanxiang America (IL)

"Frank presents legitimate ideas to rejuvenate the American economy and restore the 'American Dream.' His first-hand knowledge of communism through growing up in China, becoming an American citizen, and becoming a successful entrepreneur lends to a true world view of policies, both those that work and those that are destined to fail. Term limits and other government changes proposed by Frank would permit leaders to be elected for service rather than choosing lifetime politicians whose only concern is re-election!"

--- **Brent Jones**, GM, Henderson Machinery (NC)

"America's democracy is broken, in large part because the Republican Party is broken. American freedom-seekers need a political party that stands for all freedoms -- economic, social, cultural and political. In this regard, Frank Li's new book is an excellent source of ideas and inspiration, and is a must-read, not only for Americans, but for people the world over. Even though I might not agree with everything that Frank writes, I always find him thought-provoking. This new book is almost as brilliant as his first book."

--- **John West**, Executive Director, Asian Century Institute (Canada)

Acknowledgements

This is my second book, which turned out to be much easier than the first one. But still it was a lot of work. I am deeply indebted to several individuals for this book.

First and foremost, I would like to thank Walter Young, the legendary 91-year-old CEO of Emery Winslow Scale Company and a WWII veteran, for writing a great, personal, and passionate prologue for this book. For more about Walter, read Chapter 34.

Secondly, I would like to thank my best pen pal Jon Stimpson, President of National Scale Technology. Jon proofread most of the chapters in this book.

Special thanks go to the following individuals who provided in-book Book Reviews:
1) John Lounsbury, Ph.D.
2) Bradley Lewis, Ph.D.
3) Gary Wetzel
4) Brent Jones
5) John West.

I would like to thank John Lounsbury, the editor at GEI (Global Economic Intersection), and Steve Hansen, the publisher at GEI, for giving me a platform of publication in May 2011 and for making me a better writer over time.

Finally, I would like to thank my wife and our two sons for keeping me sane all the time. A big 'thank you' to my late father Li Dexin (Chapter 41) for giving me the good genes and upbringing that define my interest in politics and in writing, although I am an electrical engineer by training.

Prologue

Before I had the pleasure of meeting Frank Li, I heard of the Chinese man who entered our scale industry. His voice and energy were rapidly making strides. Whereas many coming from a foreign land might have walked and talked softly, Frank burst on the scene, promoting his new company, joining our scale associations, making his voice heard on major issues that affected the welfare of the American scale industry.

Today, Frank plays a major role in the affairs of the American scale industry. His voice is both powerful and respected.

However, until I reviewed his book "Saving America, Chinese Style" and his most recent book "The GOP Bible for 2016", I did not really understand that Frank had both analytical and practical wisdom far beyond what I could have imagined.

I became interested in this Chinese man, admired his business accomplishments and his forcefulness in expressing his views. I then learned that Mr. Li was also a political activist, a writer and publisher of his political views – and my interest became admiration, fully!

Having been the CEO of an industrial scale company, and then CEO and owner of a family of industrial scale companies, I fully understand the many problems faced when starting up a company and I readily admit that I depended on and required the help of many others as we began to grow our company.

Frank, on the other hand, came to our land as a graduate student, after obtaining his B.E. degree in China and his M.E degree in Japan, both in electrical engineering. He completed his education with a Ph.D. in electrical engineering from Vanderbilt University. It is an accomplishment to be admired.

After working for several companies in Europe and the U.S., Frank finally started his own company WEI (West-East International) in 2005. Today, WEI is widely recognized in the American scale industry. Another admirable accomplishment!

Frank has been a U.S. citizen for more than 15 years. For the past few years, in addition to growing his company, Frank has applied his considerable skills and energy to explain our economic free enterprise system and society in a most unique way. He articulates our political strength and weakness as only someone with his exotic background can. His personal goal of living the American Dream has indeed been achieved.

In his publications, Frank makes bold comparisons between China and America, the strengths and weaknesses of each. His comparison of Chinese versus American leaders alone (Chapters 14 and 19) is sufficient reason to read this book!

"The GOP Bible for 2016" is a splendid, and in some ways, passionate book, written intelligently and boldly. Frank takes on the American political system, expresses his contempt for the harmful liberal philosophy of the Democratic Party, and makes bold recommendations for a GOP success in 2016.

Frank Li, the man from China, now dares to lecture our politicians, as well as the American society as a whole, including a 91-year-old man like me, by advising, pleading, explaining his many complex opinions – for the good purpose of creating a more favorable future for Americans.

Through his writings, Frank demonstrates an understanding that the United States of America is still an economic and political juggernaut, with a truly multi-racial society. By virtue of his many varied experiences, his writings reflect a unique and very different point-of-view. For example, read Chapter 42 ('Everything you think you know about China is wrong', really?).

His many expressions of American vulnerability are especially telling, in some ways worrisome. I hope we will heed his advice to avoid an American tragedy in the making.

I feel certain we will hear much more from Frank in the future. Meanwhile, just read this book. It's a masterpiece, truly!

Walter Young
CEO of Emery Winslow Scale Company
Seymour, Connecticut
October 16, 2013

Introduction

The GOP is deeply in trouble, without any hope to win another presidential election in the foreseeable future! Here are four main reasons:
1) Democratic imperialism: The GOP has been too pro-war. Most Americans hate wars!
2) Religion: While the religious right supports the GOP, its positions on several major social issues (e.g. abortion) are no longer popular and are costing many votes.
3) Democratic socialism: "Democracy is the road to socialism". Who said it? Karl Marx! Because of this natural progression from democracy to socialism, the Democratic Party has been increasingly advantageous over the GOP, by attrition!
4) Ideas: To counter the natural advantage of the Democratic Party by attrition, the GOP must periodically come up with some grand new ideas that resonate with most Americans. Unfortunately, that has been missing for way too long ...

What, then, should the GOP do?

In principle, the GOP must come to the middle right, winning the middle 20% of the electorate. Specifically, the GOP must draw a stark contrast with the Democratic Party, and here it is:
1) The Democratic Party is the party of new slavery (i.e. pay without work)!
2) The GOP was the party of Lincoln who abolished slavery (i.e. work without pay) more than 150 years ago. It can again be the party to abolish new slavery from the Democratic Party today!

The image below shows my winning strategy for the GOP.

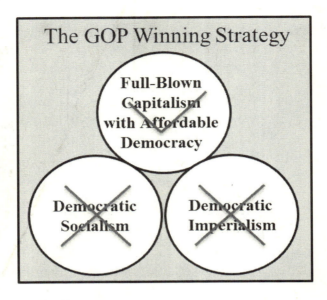

Specifically,
1) The GOP must denounce democratic imperialism, as perpetuated by the extreme right (e.g. John McCain and Lindsey Graham).
2) The GOP must denounce democratic socialism, as perpetuated by the extreme left (e.g. Nancy Pelosi and Harry Reid).
3) The GOP must be committed to restoring America as a republic with full-blown capitalism and a limited version of "affordable" democracy, largely as envisioned by our founding fathers.

This strategy will resonate with most Americans, guaranteed! Furthermore, with a great party leader in Rand Paul or Chris Christie who will be committed to this strategy, the GOP can, and will, win the 2016 presidential election, guaranteed!

This book is composed of 43 of my published articles in 2013, logically organized into a coherent whole in 10 parts as follows:
1) The GOP is dead; long live the GOP!
2) America: where are you going?
3) Correctly assessing American Presidents
4) My four open letters
5) Leadership
6) The race to the bottom
7) America: what are you doing?
8) America: a nation of self-made men!
9) America: let's have some fun!
10) Going beyond America.

Each part contains several chapters. Each chapter is an article previously published, with some significant re-writing to fit it in context. Some articles have their original publication dates attached, with the events at the time as the background.

Part 1 is the core of the book. Parts 2-4 provide the first line of support for Part 1. Parts 5-10 provide the rest of the support.

This book is available in both e-book and paperback.

This paperback is different from its sister e-book in two ways:
1) Like the e-book, the table of contents appears right after this page, without the hyper-links, of course.
2) Like the e-book, there is not a bibliography at the end of the book. Since all the references are available on-line, a reader can easily find them with a Google search by title.

Now, just sit back and enjoy the book ...

Table of Contents

Book Reviews   3
Acknowledgements   5
Prologue   6
Introduction   9
Table of Contents   12
Part 1: The GOP Is Dead; Long Live the GOP!   15
   Chapter 1: Long Live the GOP! 16
   Chapter 2: Democratic Imperialism 24
   Chapter 3: Democratic Socialism...............33
   Chapter 4: Restoring America....................38
   Chapter 5: The Democratic Party Is the Party of New Slavery! 45
Part 2: America: Where Are You Going?   52
   Chapter 6: The Coming Demise of America.............53
   Chapter 7: Top 10 American Misconceptions about Democracy...................57
   Chapter 8: Top 10 American Misconceptions about Capitalism....................62
   Chapter 9: American Exceptionalism.........66
   Chapter 10: U.S. Immigration 72
Part 3: Correctly Assessing American Presidents   76
   Chapter 11: Barack Obama vs. Harry Truman..........77
   Chapter 12: Barack Obama vs. Richard Nixon 82
   Chapter 13: Barack Obama vs. Abraham Lincoln 89
   Chapter 14: Correctly Assessing Chinese Leaders and American Presidents.................93
Part 4: My Four Open Letters   98
   Chapter 15: The First 2013 Open Letter to President Obama 99
   Chapter 16: An Open Letter to Governor Nicky Haley 107
   Chapter 17: An Open Letter to Senator Rand Paul .110

Chapter 18: My Exchanges with Senator Rand Paul 114

Part 5: Leadership 117
   Chapter 19: Top Three Leaders: the U.S. vs. China 118
   Chapter 20: The First Obama-Xi Summit 121
   Chapter 21: American Presidency: Is It a Joke (II)? 126

Part 6: The Race to the Bottom 129
   Chapter 22: Singing "the Internationale" in America? 130
   Chapter 23: Detroit, Public-Sector Unions, and JFK 134
   Chapter 24: U.S. Government Shutdown 141

Part 7: America: What Are You Doing? 144
   Chapter 25: Sequester, Capitalism, Democracy, and America 145
   Chapter 26: Patriotism: A Seventh Similarity between Communism and Democracy 150
   Chapter 27: America: What The Heck Is All This Political Correctness? 159
   Chapter 28: Money and America 163
   Chapter 29: Paul Krugman Understands Neither China Nor America! 170
   Chapter 30: Equality in America: Oversold and Overbought! 179
   Chapter 31: Jobs, Darn Jobs, and Steve Jobs 186
   Chapter 32: Who Has the Best Job in America? 192

Part 8: America: A Nation of Self-made Men! 197
   Chapter 33: Self-Made Men 198
   Chapter 34: Walter Young: A Self-Made Man! 200
   Chapter 35: Jon Stimpson: A Self-Made Man! 206
   Chapter 36: Fred Herrmann: A Self-Made Man! 210
   Chapter 37: Pin Ni: "His Own Warren Buffett" 212

Part 9: America: Let's Have Some Fun! 214
   Chapter 38: Ice Hockey: Get Rid of the Goalie! 215
   Chapter 39: Obese: to Be or Not to Be (II)? 218

Part 10: Going beyond America   223
   Chapter 40: Lee Kuan Yew 224
   Chapter 41: Li Dexin and Lee Kuan Yew 229
   Chapter 42: 'Everything You Think You Know about China is Wrong,' Really? 235
   Chapter 43: Reading "The Communist Manifesto" 240
Epilogue   243
About the Author   245

"The word politics is derived from the word 'poly', meaning 'many', and the word 'tick', meaning 'blood sucking parasites'."

--- Anonymous

"Those who are too smart to engage in politics are punished by being governed by those who are dumber."

--- Plato, 400BC

Part 1: The GOP Is Dead; Long Live the GOP!

Chapter 1: Long Live the GOP!
Chapter 2: Democratic Imperialism
Chapter 3: Democratic Socialism
Chapter 4: Restoring America
Chapter 5: The Democratic Party is the Party of New Slavery!

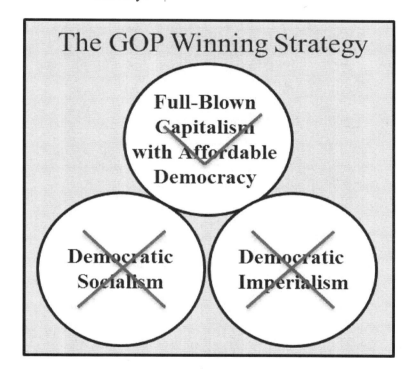

Chapter 1: Long Live the GOP!

The GOP is deeply in trouble, without any hope to win another presidential election in the foreseeable future! Many Republicans are openly worried, even John McCain (McCain: Without Immigration Reform, GOP 'Cannot Win a National Election). But nobody truly has a real answer, except for me, perhaps …

Here are my three essential messages to the GOP and America:
1) The GOP, as we know it today, is dead, without any hope to win another presidential election in the foreseeable future.
2) Without a great GOP President like Ronald Reagan soon, America will continue its steep decline towards bankruptcy.
3) The only way for the GOP to have any chance in the next presidential election is to reset itself with some grand new ideas that will resonate with most Americans. I have the ideas! But will the GOP listen?

Next, let me elaborate these three messages one by one …

1. The GOP is dead!
The GOP, as we know it today, is hopelessly dead for four main reasons:

1) Democratic imperialism: The GOP has been too pro-war. Most Americans hate wars! Specifically, the Iraq War has a lot to do with the hopelessness of the GOP today! Unfortunately, the GOP has yet to come clean on it, while praying for time to heal the wound. Worse yet, the GOP has been too deeply tangled up with the political-military complex, wasting a lot of money and even human lives in the name of saving the world, while bankrupting ourselves at home. Worst of all, since the end of the Cold War in 1989, America has actually been the major source of instability around the world in a way perhaps even worse than communism. Any doubt? Just look at Iraq, Egypt, Syria, and even Afghanistan!
2) Religion: While the religious right supports the GOP, its positions on several major social issues (e.g. abortion) are no longer popular and are costing many votes. Here is a tough reality: a long primary season often pushes the GOP to the far right, making it impossible to win the presidency in a general election in today's America!
3) Democratic socialism: "Democracy is the road to socialism" (per Karl Marx). Because of this natural progression from democracy to socialism, the Democratic Party has been increasingly advantageous over the GOP, by attrition! No, the Democratic Party needs no strategy other than this: more handouts for more votes! For example, the U.S. population receiving food stamps jumped from 28 million in 2008 to more than 46 million in 2012, a net increase of more than 18 million over President Obama's first term! Still wondering why President Obama was re-elected even after being the "food stamp President"? He was re-elected because of it!

4) Ideas: To counter the natural advantage of the Democratic Party by attrition, the GOP must periodically come up with some grand new ideas that resonate with most Americans. Unfortunately, that has been missing for way too long. It is a terrible void, or brain drain, that must be filled in order for the GOP to have any chance in the next presidential election, thus preserving our country and our way of life!

2. America needs a GOP President!

Look at the 10 most recent American Presidents (Chapter 14), all the Democrats were bad, while most of the Republicans were better, except for Bush II.

Overall, the GOP has been the real pro-business party in America, which is what America desperately needs today! No capitalism, no prosperity!

In contrast, here is a recent photo of the three living Democratic Presidents.

Do they even remotely resemble President Lincoln in any way? No! Simply put,
1) The Democratic Party is the party of new slavery (i.e. pay without work)!
2) The GOP was the party of Lincoln who abolished slavery (i.e. work without pay) more than 150 years ago. It can again be the party to abolish new slavery from the Democratic Party today!

3. The GOP needs grand new ideas!
There are fake ideas and there are real ideas.

3.1 Fake #1: Constitutionalists
One big false hope many Republicans have rests on a few constitutionalists (e.g. Speaker Boehner's Task Is To Defend The Constitution). While most constitutionalists are solid Republicans, their ideas are boring, at best, for two main reasons:
1) They are unhappy with change! They are nostalgic about the past, they ignore the present, and they have no idea about the future! So they simply want to go back to the past by waving the Constitution, despite the fact that the world has dramatically changed from the past (e.g. China's rise and the failure of American democracy).
2) They do not seem to realize that they are against the teachings of their hero, Thomas Jefferson, as shown below.

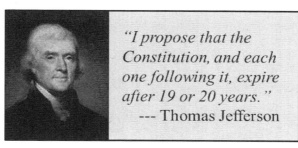

"I propose that the Constitution, and each one following it, expire after 19 or 20 years."
--- Thomas Jefferson

In other words, it has been right for America to amend its Constitution over the past 200 plus years. Unfortunately,
1) Some amendments were wrong (e.g. changing the top political offices from unpaid to paid).
2) Some items in the original Constitution are simply out of date, such as the minimum age for the American Presidency which remains at 35 (American Presidency: Raising the Minimum Age to 55!).
3) We must have a new amendment: term-limits for Congress!

3.2 Fake #2: John McCain

Here is a recent message from John McCain: Without Immigration Reform, GOP 'Cannot Win a National Election'. This message is basically correct, in the absence of some grand new ideas for the GOP. But McCain's solution of endorsing the Immigration Bill will be even worse for the GOP! Here is an excerpt from Chapter 6 ("The Coming Demise of America"):

In the current era, overwhelming majorities of immigrants are Democrats, by definition!

If the Hispanic vote made the difference in the 2012 presidential election, it will be the eternal difference after the Immigration Bill is passed, which means the days of having a pro-business American President are gone, forever!

Now, read this: John McCain on Hillary Clinton or Rand Paul? 'Tough Choice'. Is McCain a Republican at all? No, he is not – He is a RINO (Republican In Name Only), just like Lindsey Graham! Or more accurately, McCain is simply Republican for a few months every six years, during his re-election campaigns. His constituents, like sheep, are easily led!

3.3 Real ideas

In principle, the GOP must come to the middle right, winning the middle 20% of the electorate by having some grand new ideas.

The image below shows my winning strategy for the GOP.

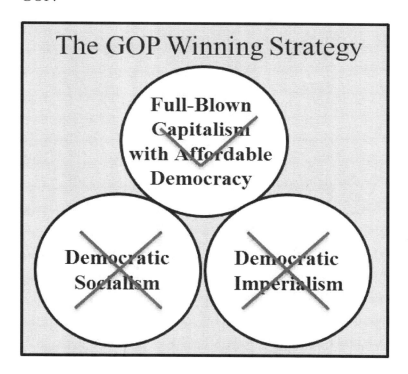

Specifically,
1) The GOP must denounce democratic imperialism, as perpetuated by the extreme right (e.g. John McCain and Lindsey Graham). For more, read Chapter 2 ("Democratic Imperialism").

2) The GOP must denounce democratic socialism, as perpetuated by the extreme left (e.g. Nancy Pelosi and Harry Reid). For more, read Chapter 3 ("Democratic Socialism").
3) The GOP must be committed to restoring America as a republic with full-blown capitalism and a limited version of "affordable" democracy, largely as envisioned by our founding fathers. For more, read Chapter 4 ("Restoring America").

With that, all that the GOP needs is a strong leader who will buy into this strategy!

4. Who should be the next GOP leader?
Both Senator Rand Paul and Governor Chris Christie are excellent candidates to be the next American President! How to choose between the two? Apply, if not demand, a litmus test as follows:
1) He must promise to be a one-term (i.e. four years) President, without fooling around for his own re-election!
2) He must promise to have significant constitutional changes as I suggested. For example, set term-limits for all the top political offices, starting with the American Presidency to be one-term (e.g. six years); and raise the statutory requirements for the President (e.g. age 55 and having served as a state governor for one full-term at least).

For details, read my book: <u>Saving America, Chinese Style</u>.

With these real ideas and a strong leader, the GOP can, and will, resonate with most Americans, thus winning the 2016 presidential election, guaranteed!

5. Closing

History is written by heroic individuals. In China, there was Deng, who proved to be one of the greatest peaceful transformational leaders in human history. America is desperately in need of her own heroic leader like China's Deng. That person can only come from the GOP!

I conditionally endorsed Senator Rand Paul on 3/21/2013 (Chapter 17: "An Open Letter to Senator Rand Paul"). I welcome Governor Chris Christie to the race. But will either rise to the occasion? Let's wait and see …

Chapter 2: Democratic Imperialism

What is democratic imperialism?

Google it and you will have many results, from articles (e.g. Democratic Imperialism: A Blueprint) to books (e.g. Democratic Imperialism: A Book about Democracy Promotion). However, there is no definition in Wikipedia, yet. For this reason, as well as for its importance to this book, let me clearly define it here.

1. Imperialism: what is it?
According to Wikipedia:

> **Imperialism**, as defined by the Dictionary of Human Geography, is "an unequal human and territorial relationship, usually in the form of an empire, based on ideas of superiority and practices of dominance, and involving the extension of authority and control of one state or people over another."[2] It is often considered in a negative light, as merely the exploitation of native people in order to enrich a small handful.[3] Lewis Samuel Feuer identifies two major subtypes of imperialism; the first is the "regressive imperialism" identified with pure conquest, unequivocal exploitation, extermination or reductions of undesired peoples, and settlement of desired peoples into those territories, examples

being Nazi Germany.[4] The second type identified by Feuer is "progressive imperialism" that is founded upon a cosmopolitan view of humanity, that promotes the spread of civilization to allegedly "backward" societies to elevate living standards and culture in conquered territories, and allowance of a conquered people to assimilate into the imperial society, examples being the Roman Empire and the British Empire.[4]

The term as such primarily has been applied to Western political and economic dominance in the 19th and 20th centuries. Some writers, such as Edward Said, use the term more broadly to describe any system of domination and subordination organized with an imperial center and a periphery.[citation needed] According to the Marxist historian, Walter Rodney, imperialism meant capitalist expansion. It meant that European (and American and Japanese) capitalists were forced by the internal logic of their competitive system to seek abroad in less developed countries opportunities to control raw material, to find markets, and to find profitable fields of investment. [citation needed]

Here is my simple and succinct definition: imperialism today is to support and/or launch a war in a foreign land for the purpose of some perceived gain at home, such as boosting popularity for an election.

2. Democracy: what is it?
According to Wikipedia,

Democracy is a form of government in which all citizens have an equal say in the decisions that affect their lives. Democracy allows citizens to participate equally—either directly or through elected representatives—in the proposal, development, and creation of laws. It encompasses social, economic and cultural conditions that enable the free and equal practice of political self-determination.

Here is my simple and succinct definition: one person, one vote.

3. Democratic imperialism: what is it?
Here is my succinct definition:

Democratic imperialism is imperialism practiced by a democracy for the purpose of spreading democracy. While practiced by the U.S. for many years, it obviously and officially became imperialistic on March 20, 2003, when the U.S. launched the Iraq War. It has continued since then, with America's military intervention in Libya and Syria being the latest examples.

3.1 Democratic imperialism under President Bush II
President George W. Bush's legacy is unquestionably defined by the Iraq War, which was such a huge disaster that the following three writings depict it in some ways:
1) Hubris: The Inside Story of Spin, Scandal, and the Selling of the Iraq War.
2) What's The Real Cost of The Iraq War?
3) Thomas Young, Dying Iraq War veteran, Pens 'Last Letter" to Bush, Cheney On War's 10th Anniversary.

3.2 Democratic imperialism under President Obama

The Nobel Peace Prize 2009 was awarded to President Obama *"for his extraordinary efforts to strengthen international diplomacy and cooperation between peoples"* (The Noble Peace Prize 2009).

Unfortunately for the world, President Obama has proven to be a bad democratic imperialist too, even worse than his predecessor in some ways. Three examples:

1) His 2009 speech in Cairo (President Obama Speech to Muslim World in Cairo) has turned out to be a significant "inciting" cause behind the Arab Spring, resulting in huge chaos and misery in the Middle East today, particularly in Egypt. The

Arab Spring will prove to be a disaster, just like the communist revolution in China in 1949. For more, read: American Autumn vs. Arab Spring.
2) He escalated the war in Afghanistan in 2011, at least partially, for the sake of his re-election. For more, read: For Obama the Road to Reelection Runs through Kabul.
3) He got America involved in two new wars in Libya and Syria (Breaking News: Every Military Option in Syria Sucks)!

In short, President Obama has tainted the Noble Peace Prize, which should not have been awarded to him in the first place - He did not earn it!

Now, as you may know already, my diagnosis for America is cancer: getting re-elected *ad nauseam*. So here is a valid question: why did President Obama get us involved in the war in Syria recently, as he has no re-election of his own anymore?

Read this: Obama's Top Goal: For Dems To Win The House In 2014.

To hell with governing - Only elections count to our politicians, including President Obama!

4. Democracy = Opium?

As a Chinese who was well educated about the two Opium Wars, let me draw two simple analogies between democracy and opium as follows:
1) Both democracy and opium can make you feel good for a while.
2) Both democracy and opium are harmful, even fatal, in the long run.

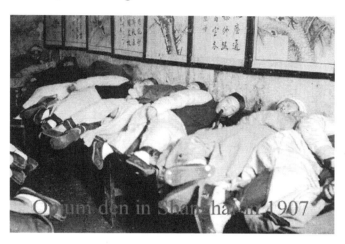

Opium den in Shanghai in 1907

Harvesting "democratic" opium in Afghanistan in 2012

If a war for selling opium was imperialistic, a war for selling democracy is also imperialistic! Therefore, the Iraq War was imperialistic. Because it was the first huge war ever launched by a democracy specifically for the purpose of spreading democracy, let's call it by its proper name: democratic imperialism!

The same logic applies to the wars in Libya and Syria.

5. More on democracy
America has been spreading democracy in the Middle East by all means, including wars. Three basic questions:
1) Is democracy working over there? No! Here is a recent news story from Egypt: Egypt declares national emergency.
2) Is the change to democracy in Egypt good for America? No! Here is a recent article: Egypt, U.S. on Collision Course. Here is a recent picture from Egypt:

3) Will democracy ever work in Egypt? No, not in my life time at least! Here is an excerpt from my last book (Saving America, Chinese Style):

> *The #1 problem in the Middle East is abject poverty, for which the only solution is capitalism, not democracy! As a matter of fact, there is not a single example of success for a third-world country achieving prosperity via democracy!*

Bottom line: democracy does not work over there! Worse yet, it's democracy that has been a key reason behind the huge chaos, misery, and massive killings over there! Specifically,
1) The Iraqis were much better off under Saddam than today! President George W. Bush is directly responsible for the mess in Iraq, obviously!
2) The Egyptians were much better off under Mubarak than today! President Obama is directly responsible for the mess in Egypt! Not so obvious? Watch this video: President Obama Speech to Muslim World in Cairo in 2009, review the events since then, and think …

Now, a bigger question for my fellow Americans: what about democracy at home? No, it no longer works here either! For more, read Chapter 6 ("The Coming Demise of America")!

Exporting something, an ideology or a product, that does not even work at home, by force? What the hell do we think we are doing? What the hell is this thing called [American] democracy?

6. What's America, anyway?

America was built as a republic with full-blown capitalism and a limited version of democracy! However, over the past 200 years, America has progressively amended the U.S. Constitution to morph itself into a full-blown democracy (i.e. <u>one person, one vote</u>), against the wisdom of the founding fathers!

As a result, America is being destroyed by democratic imperialism, as well as democratic socialism (Chapter 3).

7. Closing

For most Americans, democratic imperialism is far worse than democratic socialism. Therefore, the GOP must be anti-war by denouncing democratic imperialism, immediately and forcefully, in order to have any chance in the next presidential election and beyond! Specifically, expel the war hawks like John McCain and Lindsey Graham from the GOP, immediately! They are RINOs (Republicans In Name Only), anyway!

Chapter 3: Democratic Socialism

Unlike democratic imperialism, which has yet to have a definition in Wikipedia, democratic socialism is already defined in Wikipedia.

1. Democratic socialism: Wikipedia's definition
According to Wikipedia,

> **Democratic socialism** is a variant of socialism that rejects centralized, elitist, or authoritarian methods of transitioning from capitalism to socialism in favor of grassroots-level movements aiming for the immediate creation of decentralized economic democracy.
>
> The term is often used by socialists who favor either electoral transition to socialism or a spontaneous mass revolution from below to distinguish themselves from authoritarian socialists that call for a single-party state, most notably to contrast with Stalinists and Maoists.
>
> Democratic socialists endorse a post-capitalist, socialist economic system as an alternative to capitalism. Some democratic socialists advocate market socialism based on workplace self-management, while others support a non-market system based on decentralized-participatory

planning. Many contemporary democratic socialists reject centralized planning as a basis for democratic socialism.

Unfortunately, after all the words above, Wikipedia concludes the definition in this way: "Democratic socialism is difficult to define, and groups of scholars have radically different definitions for the term."

In other words, it is whatever you want to use it as!

2. Democratic socialism: my definition

For its importance to this book, let me clearly define "democratic socialism in the U.S." as follows:

> Democratic socialism in the U.S. is socialism as epitomized by the social policies of the Democratic Party, which is aimed at having a bigger and bigger government, more and more dependence (e.g. food stamps), and more and more stupid, or poorly informed, supplicants who vote only for the Democratic Party.

The image below highlights this definition.

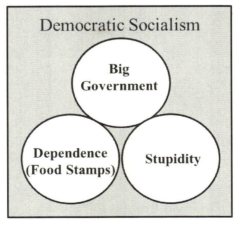

Now, let me elaborate the three circles one by one.

2.1 Big government

Read: <u>Government Employees and Manufacturing Jobs: Takers and Makers?</u> Here is an excerpt,

> *In 2011, there are nearly twice as many people working for the government (22.5 million) than in all of the manufacturing (11.5 million). This is almost exact reversal of the situation in 1960, when there were 15 million workers in manufacturing and 8.8 million collecting a paycheck from the government ... More Americans work for the government than work in construction, farming, fishing, manufacturing, mining, and utilities combined. We have moved decisively from a nation of makers to a nation of takers.*

In short, we have become a nation of takers!

2.2 Dependence

With the present expenditures of over $4 trillion/year by the U.S. government and a population of 315 million, we are spending over $13,000/year/person on just the federal level! Add in state and local and it approaches $18,000/year/person. So anyone paying less than $18,000 per year in taxes is a "taker" and someone else is paying their "fair share." For a family of four, that's $72,000/year in taxes they must pay to be a "maker" instead of a taker.

Now, let's look at the food stamps. As shown by the chart below, the U.S. population receiving food stamps jumped from 28 million in 2008 to more than 46 million in 2012, a net increase of more than 18 million over President Obama's first term!

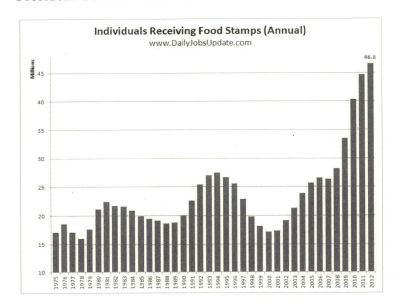

What's the implication of food stamps? Here is a "joke" widely circulated on the Internet:

> *The Food Stamp Program, administered by the U.S. Department of Agriculture, is proud to be distributing, this year, the greatest amount of free meals and food stamps ever, to 46 million people. Meanwhile, the National Park Service, administered by the U.S. Department of the Interior, asks us "Please Do Not Feed the Animals." Their stated reason for the policy is because "The animals will grow dependent on handouts and will not learn to take care of themselves."*

Get it? I hope you do …

2.3 Stupidity

Watch this video: Obama is going to pay for my gas and mortgage. Known as "parasites" in many parts of the world (e.g. in China), these people can vote in America. Worse yet, there are so many of them now that they can even decide the outcome of a presidential election!

Need more evidence that many Americans have become dumber? Read this: U.S. adults are dumber than the average human.

For more, read: Stupidity: A Sixth Similarity between Communism and Democracy.

3. Closing

American politicians work for one predominant purpose only: getting re-elected *ad nauseam*. The Democratic Party is better off, in terms of winning elections, with a bigger government, more food stamps, and more stupid voters!

"Both career politicians and career welfare recipients are parasites. Together, we have been destroying America from inside out!"

--- Frank Li

America must be restored as the "Land of Opportunity", where you are expected to work hard, produce results, and be richly and fairly rewarded! For more, proceed to the next chapter …

Chapter 4: Restoring America

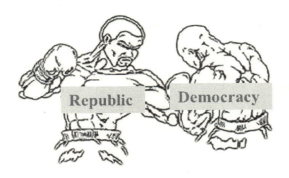

Restoring America must start with an in-depth discussion of this subject: "republic vs. democracy".

Google "republic vs. democracy" and you will get a lot of results. Most are interesting, but not sufficiently forthright.

Here is a recent article: Republic vs. Democracy. It's interesting because it provides, in its title, a clear confrontation between republic (i.e. "free from things public") and democracy (i.e. "a mob for a king"). But like many other publications, it's not forthright.

Allow me to provide my version of republic vs. democracy, focusing on America.

1. Definitions

1.1 Republic
According to Wikipedia,

> A **republic** is a form of government in which the country is considered a "public matter" (Latin: res publica), not the private concern or property

of the rulers, and where offices of states are subsequently directly or indirectly elected or appointed rather than inherited. In modern times, a common simplified definition of a republic is a government where the head of state is not a monarch.[1][2].

In modern republics such as the United States, Russia, and India, the executive is legitimized both by a constitution and by popular suffrage. Montesquieu included both democracies, where all the people have a share in rule, and aristocracies or oligarchies, where only some of the people rule, as republican forms of government.[4]

Here is my simple definition: today, if you are not a monarchy, you are a republic, with or without democracy.

No, the term "republic" does not mean much these days. Three examples:
1) China calls itself "The People's Republic of China", without democracy.
2) America, according to Wikipedia, is still a republic, with democracy.
3) North Korea calls itself "Democratic People's Republic of Korea", which, in reality, neither has democracy nor is a republic. It is a *de facto* monarchy, with a son succeeding the father as the "king".

1.2 Democracy

Again, as defined in Chapter 2 ("Democratic Imperialism"), democracy is one person, one vote.

2. America and democracy

America was built as a republic (i.e. non-monarchy), and it remains a republic today. The difference between 200 years ago and today is democracy. Democracy, by the simple but strict definition of <u>one person, one vote</u>, did not exist in the U.S. until 1964, when <u>one person, one vote</u> finally became a reality in America.

The founding fathers never intended America to be a democracy! For proof, look at these two sources:
1) The U.S. Constitution.
2) The thoughts and words of the founding fathers.

2.1 The U.S. Constitution

"We, the People", so begins the U.S. Constitution. But who are "the People" referenced? To the founding fathers, "the People" included only certain rich white men as follows:
1) Women were not allowed to vote, nor were the minorities.
2) Only the rich were able to serve since all the top political offices (e.g. Congress and the American Presidency) were unpaid! Yes, first you had to make it (i.e. being financially independent), then you served with honor for a few years, and finally you returned home after doing your duty to your country. No, serving was never meant to be a way of life - not even to make a living, let alone a career!

Why didn't the founding fathers simply set up America as a democracy with one person, one vote? Apparently, they did not believe in democracy! Why not? Here is what we know for sure: history by then (and now) was replete with failures of democracies, without a single example of lasting success!

What, then, is a lasting success? How about 200 years? Isn't America more than 200 years old already? Yes! But American democracy is less than 50 years old (from 1964 to present), and it is already crumbling, badly, destroying America faster and better than any other forces!

2.2 Founding fathers' words
Two examples:

"Remember, democracy never lasts long. It soon wastes, exhausts, and murders itself. There never was a democracy yet that did not commit suicide."
--- John Adams

"A democracy is nothing more than mob rule, where fifty-one-percent of the people may take away the rights of the other forty-nine."
--- Thomas Jefferson

3. American democracy

Over the past 200 plus years, America has progressively amended the U.S. Constitution to morph itself into a democracy (i.e. one person, one vote), against the wisdom of the founding fathers, resulting in America being on a "suicide" path today, exactly as predicted by John Adams more than 200 years ago.

Here is my take on American democracy:
1) The founding fathers were all experienced and wise men. But no human being could have been so foresighted as to see everything more than 200 years ahead!
2) Discrimination against race or gender, as in the original U.S. Constitution, was patently wrong.
3) It was right to set the top political offices to be unpaid positions, so that you had to make it first before being eligible to serve at the top.
4) It is time to have substantial and specific constitutional changes to give American democracy a chance to survive before it dies in the same way as democracy died in ancient Rome and ancient Greece more than 2,000 years ago: debts!

4. U.S. Constitutional changes

Here are 10-point changes I proposed in my book (Saving America, Chinese Style):
1) Setting term-limits for the top elected offices:
    - President: One term (e.g. six years), firm!
    - Senator: Six years per term. One term, preferably.
    - House of Representatives: Six years per term. One term, preferably.
2) Raising the statutory requirements for the Presidency, such as the minimum age to 55 and

having served as a state governor for one full-term, at least.
3) Abolishing the Electoral College! Just count votes, instead!
4) Spending must be controlled!
   - Limiting spending to a certain percentage of the GDP (e.g. 15%).
   - The budget must be balanced. If there is potential of growth, some deficit is allowed. However, always figure out how to pay for it first before introducing any new big spending program.
   - Cutting the defense spending drastically. If not, we will soon have no country left to defend!
5) Minimizing the government, with the understanding that government does not create real jobs in quantity. The private sector does!
6) Dissolving all public-sector unions immediately and banning them forever, with an executive order to undo President Kennedy's Executive Order 10988.
7) Reforming Social Security and Medicare. Abolishing all entitlement programs (e.g. Medicaid) and replacing them with a minimal welfare system. **Bottom line**: No one should be better off on welfare than they are by working! To be more specific, the welfare benefit must not exceed half of the minimum wage!
8) Simplifying everything, from laws to the tax code, so as to reduce the number of lawyers and accountants. Most importantly, you don't have to be a lawyer to run for office.
9) Yes, a voter ID is a must, just like driving or drinking!
10) Raising the minimum voting age to 21, so that voting is at least as important as drinking!

5. Closing

America must be restored as a country with full-blown capitalism and a limited version of affordable democracy!

Barring a bloody revolution, the only way for America to restore itself is to have a great transformational American President. This President can only come from the GOP, because the Democratic Party is truly the party of new slavery! For more, proceed to the next chapter.

Chapter 5: The Democratic Party Is the Party of New Slavery!

In this chapter, I will explicitly point out that the Democratic Party is the party of new slavery! I will do it by providing a harsh clear look at the history of the Democratic Party.

1. What is the Democratic Party?

Here is how Wikipedia highlights the Democratic Party:

> The **Democratic Party** is one of the two major contemporary political parties in the United States along with the Republican Party. Since the 1930s, the party has promoted a socially liberal and progressive platform,[2][3][4] and its Congressional caucus is composed of progressives, liberals, and centrists.[5] The party has the lengthiest record of continuous operation in the United States and is probably the oldest political party in the world.[6]

Because the highlight describes the Democratic Party from the 1930s on, my harsh look will be from the 1930s on as well. For a more thorough definition of the Democratic Party, read: Wikipedia's whole definition of the Democratic Party.

2. Why is it the party of new slavery?
The Democratic Party promotes democratic socialism (Chapter 3), which means *"a bigger and bigger government, more and more government dependence (e.g. food stamps), and more and more stupid, or poorly informed, supplicants who vote only for the Democratic Party"*.

The old form of slavery: work without pay. The new form of slavery: pay without work! The outcome of the two forms of slavery is the same: human deprivation!

INDEPENDENCE = FREEDOM
DEPENDENCE = SLAVERY

Now, let's revisit the issue of food stamps (Chapter 3: "Democratic Socialism"). What is the party affiliation of the food stamp recipients? Read: The politics and demographics of food stamp recipients. Here is an excerpt:

> *Democrats are about twice as likely as Republicans to have received food stamps at some point in their lives—a participation gap that echoes the deep partisan divide in the U.S.*

For more, go back to Chapter 3 ("Democratic Socialism")!

3. How did it become the party of new slavery?
Getting re-elected *ad nauseam*!

Because the Republican Party represents the rich in general, the Democratic Party goes after the poor in general. In other words, the more the poor, the better off for the Democratic Party, especially in terms of winning elections!

Specifically, let's look at the Democratic American Presidents from the 1930s on ...

3.1 FDR
FDR faced formidable challenges (e.g. The Great Depression) when he was elected to the American Presidency. He did everything possible to remain popular, in order to be re-elected again and again (yes, three times), even if it meant raiding the public treasury by initiating various big social programs. Two examples:
1) New Deal: This was the beginning of America as an entitlement society vs. unfettered capitalism based on rugged individualism.
2) Social Security: It is not an entitlement program *per se*, especially for those who have paid into it. Rather, it's a Ponzi scheme predestined to fail! In fact, it is such a big Ponzi scheme that it makes Bernie Madoff look trivial.

In short, FDR led America into democratic socialism big time, which has only been progressively getting worse since then, with the government getting so big and fat now that its massive weight is crushing America.

3.2 Harry Truman
President Truman was an exception – He did not initiate any big social program that would damage America down the road! Why not? Maybe he was too busy with the wars (i.e. WWII and the Korean War). Maybe FDR did too much already. Maybe he decided

early on not to run for re-election in 1952 (Why_didn't_Truman_run_for_reelection_in_1952?). Or maybe he was just a good man!

For more on President Truman, read Chapter 11 ("Barack Obama vs. Harry Truman").

3.3 JFK

JFK will eventually be recognized as the worst American President, ever! Why? In 1961, he issued Executive Order 10988, allowing the public-sector workers to unionize against the United Stated of America!

Public-sector unions are not just socialistic – They are communistic! For more, read: Chapter 23 ("Detroit, Public-Sector Unions, and JFK").

3.4 LBJ

LBJ was a big socialist who led America more deeply into democratic socialism, following FDR, via more social programs. Two examples:
1) Medicare and Medicaid: We have been borrowing to pay for them since their inception! Like Social Security, Medicare is not an entitlement program *per se*, but a Ponzi scheme. Medicaid, on the other hand, is simply an entitlement program.

2) Great Society: This is the official big-time start of new slavery in America: pay without work! It has such a big detrimental effect on American society that many of today's social problems can be traced to it. For example, look at the daily street killings in Chicago in recent years ... What's the root cause? Guns? No! It's the break-down of America's core values, from families (e.g. single-parent vs. two-parents) to work ethic (e.g. pay without work). Yes, pay without work is an insidious form of human deprivation, especially in the long-run! It is finally showing up big time now, with the far worse yet to come!

Now, on the Civil Rights movement ... Here is an excerpt from Chapter 30 ("Equality in America: Oversold and Overbought!"):

With one person, one vote becoming a reality as a result of the Civil Rights movement, America was fundamentally changed from a republic with full-blown capitalism and a limited-version of democracy to full-blown democracy and an increasingly crippled version of capitalism, totally against the wisdom of the founding fathers!

3.5 Jimmy Carter

President Carter was simply a bomb! One example: Community Reinvestment Act (CRA). It was the key factor in the creation of the housing bubble that burst in 2008.

3.6 Bill Clinton

President Clinton was the luckiest American President until President Obama! He amended the CRA to its final, and lethal, form, thus contributing to a spectacular housing bubble that burst in 2008. For more, read: <u>The Myth of The Bill Clinton Presidency</u>.

3.7 Barack Obama

President Obama is the only American that has made both lists of mine: democratic imperialists (Chapter 2) and democratic socialists (Chapter 3)!

What about Obamacare? It will prove to be a drainer to our economy, just like Medicare/Medicaid!

4. Discussion

Americans must understand these four key points:
1) Democracy (i.e. <u>one person, one vote</u>) is a proven failure in human history (e.g. ancient Rome and ancient Greece). It was largely for this reason that America was founded as a republic with full-blown capitalism and a limited version of democracy (i.e. specifically without one person, one vote), thanks to the extraordinary wisdom of our founding fathers! Unfortunately, over the past 200 years, America has progressively amended the U.S. Constitution to morph itself into a full-blown democracy (i.e. one person, one vote) and an increasingly crippled version of capitalism, resulting in so much trouble today, with no easy way out!
2) Communism is also a proven failure in human history. Democracy, as we practice it today, looks more and more like communism, especially the SFN (or "something for nothing") part - <u>Been there, done that</u>! It will therefore fail, just like communism did!
3) Both ancient democracy and communism failed for the same reason: Debts! They destroyed the rich and they all died poor.

4) Who are the Democrats in the U.S. today? "Most of them are socialists, with the extreme left being communists!" For more, read Chapter 6 ("The Coming Demise of America").

5. Closing

America is deeply in trouble because of democracy, as we practice it today! The driving force behind American democracy has been the Democratic Party, whose social policy has resulted in a new form of slavery: pay without work. It is an insidious form of human deprivation!

It's time for Americans to recognize the Democratic Party as the party of new slavery!

Unless the GOP can get better soon as I suggested (Chapter 1: "Long live the GOP!"), America will continue its steep decline towards another type of slavery: debt slavery!

Part 2: America: Where Are You Going?

Chapter 6: The Coming Demise of America
Chapter 7: Top 10 American Misconceptions about Democracy
Chapter 8: Top 10 American Misconceptions about Capitalism
Chapter 9: American Exceptionalism
Chapter 10: U.S. Immigration

"The answer is democracy; the question is why."
--- Frank Li

Chapter 6: The Coming Demise of America
(Initially published at GEI on 7/4/2013)

Happy birthday, America! This is the best possible gift I can give America, today.

Let me clearly point out one harsh reality: with Obamacare kicking in and with the Immigration Bill imminent, the GOP is becoming increasingly irrelevant and may never win another presidential election. Consequently, America will no longer have a truly pro-business President. Democracy will kill capitalism in America, and hence America …

1. Understanding America: yesterday

Most Americans have been programmed to believe that America, the most powerful country on earth today, has two cornerstones: capitalism and democracy, as illustrated below.

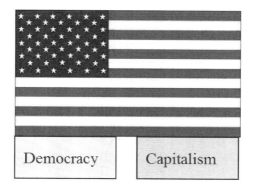

2. Understanding America: today

Democracy is not a cornerstone for America at all - Capitalism is the sole building block! In other words, capitalism is the foundation not only for America, but also for democracy, as illustrated below.

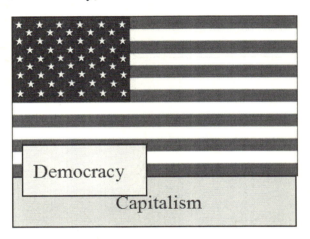

3. Understanding America: tomorrow

When democracy gets too big and too distorted, it will crush the foundation, resulting in a catastrophic collapse of America, as further illustrated below.

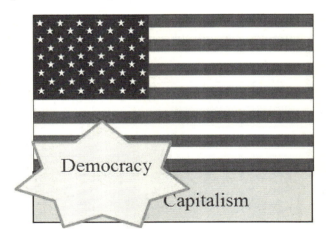

4. Democracy vs. capitalism

Here are two important chapters coming:
1) Chapter 7: "Top 10 American Misconceptions about Democracy".
2) Chapter 8: "Top 10 American Misconceptions about Capitalism".

Bottom line: no capitalism, no prosperity!

5. No capitalism, no prosperity

The 2012 election provided one ominous sign to America: the electorate has become too dependent on government handouts to tolerate a President who does not offer more of the same. In other words, America has become too Democratic to have a non-Democrat as the President!

What, then, are the Democrats? Most of them are socialists, with the extreme left being communists!

Regrettably for America, this ominous sign will become more immutable after Obamacare kicks in and will become permanent with the coming Immigration Bill, regardless of its final form! Why? In the current era, overwhelming majorities of immigrants are Democrats, by definition!

If the Hispanic vote made the difference in the 2012 presidential election, it will be the eternal difference after the Immigration Bill is passed, which means the days of having a truly pro-business American President are gone, forever!

Yes, democracy will kill capitalism in America, and hence America!

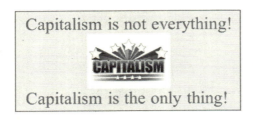

6. Saving America, my way ...

I love America! To thank America, my adopted country, maximally, I want to save it with my pen (or keyboard, to be more precise)!

Last year for America's birthday, I published this article: Four Points to Ponder on America's 236th Birthday. I recently reviewed it – not a single word needs to be changed!

This year, I have added something much better: my book: Saving America, Chinese Style. Here is what I have done with this book: I mailed autographed copies to many VIPs. I will keep you posted if I hear back from any of them.

7. Closing

We must change the course if we are to leave a viable country to our children!

My proposal (Saving America, Chinese Style) is the best on the table. Americans will buy my diagnosis and solution, if more people will listen ...

Chapter 7: Top 10 American Misconceptions about Democracy

America is a very young country (as compared with China, for example) and Americans often take many old things as new, innocently and ignorantly. Two examples:
1) Fiat money: It was invented by the Chinese more than 1,000 years ago!
2) Money printing: It has been used, misused, and abused, by many governments around the world ever since fiat money was invented.

However, no old-as-new has been more damaging to America than democracy, which was invented by the Romans and Greeks more than 2,000 years ago. Both of them ultimately failed for the same reason: debts!

In short, democracy is a proven failure in human history!

Now, let me highlight the top 10 American misconceptions about democracy (i.e. one person, one vote).

Misconception 1: The U.S. has been a democracy since her inception

The U.S. has been loosely called a democracy since her inception on July 4, 1776. However, by the simple but succinct definition of one person, one vote, democracy did not exist in the U.S. until 1964.

Misconception 2: The U.S. was built as a democracy

The U.S. was not built as a democracy! Instead, the U.S. was built as a republic with full-blown capitalism and a limited version of democracy, specifically without one person, one vote! For more, read Chapter 4 ("Restoring America").

Misconception 3: The founding fathers meant the U.S. to be a democracy

The founding fathers never intended the U.S. to be a democracy! For more, go back to Chapter 4 ("Restoring America").

Misconception 4: The U.S. leads mankind in democracy

Democracy was invented and practiced by the Romans and Greeks more than 2,000 years ago. Both ultimately failed for the same reason: debts!

Misconception 5: Democracy has succeeded in America

Although American democracy is less than 50 years old (i.e. from 1964 to present), it is already failing badly, destroying America faster and harsher than any other forces!

> "America will never be destroyed from the outside. If we falter and lose our freedoms, it will be because we destroyed ourselves."
> --- Abraham Lincoln

Worse yet, democracy is failing in America today in the same way as it failed in Rome and Greece more than 2,000 years ago: debts!

Misconception 6: America's government is of/by/for the people

Think again! Three perspectives:

1) Are our children and their children people too? If yes, do you still think it right that we spend their financial futures like there is no tomorrow?
2) If Congress is of/by/for the people, why is its disapproval rate at 87% among Americans?
3) What about the President? We elect/re-elect one every four years with about 50% of the votes. We complain about him for four years until the next election. Meanwhile, he is most likely to damage America a lot for the sake of his own re-election or of some other elections of his own party. For more, read Part 3 ("Correctly Assessing American Presidents").

Misconception 7: Democracy is not perfect but it's still the best system available

Most Americans blindly believe in democracy, thanks, in a large part, to brainwashing, although more and more Americans acknowledge that "our democracy is broken" (e.g. on guns or debts). Here is a pertinent fact: democracy is not broken; today, American democracy works exactly according to its script of more than 2,000 years old. Unfortunately, the script is a proven failure. Therefore, American democracy, as we practice it today, is hopelessly doomed!

On the other hand, the Chinese system (i.e. capitalism + autocracy), albeit with many endemic problems of its own, appears to be slightly better than democracy. For more, read my book: Saving America, Chinese Style!

Misconception 8: Democracy is a cornerstone for America

Democracy is not a cornerstone for America! Capitalism is! Democracy is merely a nice-to-have luxury. America can no longer afford this luxury! For more, read Chapter 6 ("The Coming Demise of America").

Bottom line: "the political system does not matter, as long as it embraces capitalism," which is the key difference between the U.S. and China today (Saving America, Chinese Style)!

Misconception 9: America has been rightfully spreading democracy

America has been spreading democracy all over the world, even by force as in the case of Iraq. But it has always been dead wrong! For more, read Chapter 2 ("Democratic Imperialism").

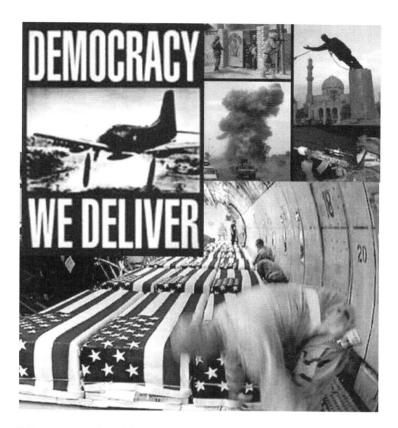

Misconception 10: American democracy is finished

Not yet! American democracy, as we practice it today, must be substantially and specifically reformed, as I suggested (Saving America, Chinese Style), in order to have a chance to survive!

Chapter 8: Top 10 American Misconceptions about Capitalism

In this chapter, I will highlight the top 10 American misconceptions about capitalism.

Misconception 1: Capitalism is evil
Capitalism is not evil! Capitalism is the best thing that ever happened to mankind! Capitalism creates unprecedented prosperity!

Misconception 2: Capitalism is not working
Capitalism works wherever it is allowed, even in "Communist" China today!

It was capitalism that propelled the West ahead of China about 200 years ago (America: What is China, Anyway?). It is capitalism that has got some 500 million Chinese out of abject poverty over the past three decades, in a fashion totally unprecedented in human history!

Misconception 3: Capitalism is perfect
Capitalism is imperfect! While we all should embrace free market and trickle-down economics, crony capitalism must be condemned and crony capitalists like Bernie Madoff must be brought to justice.

Misconception 4: Capitalism is great for everyone

Unlike democracy, which claims to treat people equally, capitalism treats you differently according to your ability (and luck). For more, read: Politics & Economics: Pyramid Theory I.

Over the past 200 years, the U.S. has produced more billionaires than everywhere else in the world, combined! Three examples: Thomas Edison, Henry Ford, and Steve Jobs. They worked hard, obtained fantastic results, and were richly and fairly rewarded!

Today, despite all its problems, the U.S. remains the best on earth as the "Land of Opportunity"!

Misconception 5: Blame the top 1% for the bad U.S. economy

Do not blame the top 1% - join them! Want to have a good life? Work for it, or go without! For more, read Part 8 ("America: A Nation of Self-Made Men").

Misconception 6: Occupy Wall Street was legitimate

Occupy Wall Street was communistic! However, we might have some sympathy for many occupiers who were victims of a moribund economy. Specifically,
1) Who caused the bad U.S. economy? Democracy, as we practice it today! For example, the real

culprit behind the housing bubble that burst in 2008 was, and still is, Community Reinvestment Act!
2) What's the solution? As a start, term-limits for the top political offices, with the American Presidency being one-term! For more, read my book: Saving America, Chinese Style!
3) Where is the right place to protest? Washington D.C.! Our politicians fiddling with free market capitalism caused the Great Recession!

Misconception 7: Blame capitalism for the bad U.S. economy

Do not blame capitalism! Rather, blame democracy, as we practice it today!

Here is a relevant quote: "Democracy is the road to socialism". Who said it? Karl Marx (The Communist Manifesto's Road to Socialism through democracy)!

Misconception 8: Capitalism cannot be destroyed

Capitalism will not self-destruct. Socialism, the arch-rival of capitalism, will destroy it. Socialism can happen not only via communism but also via democracy. As a matter of fact, democracy looks more and more like communism (Saving America, Chinese Style).

Misconception 9: Capitalism and democracy go hand in hand

Capitalism was, and still is, the cornerstone for America. Democracy is merely a nice-to-have luxury. America can no longer afford this luxury! Democracy, as we practice today, has been crushing capitalism in America!

China has no democracy. Yet, capitalism is working well over there!

"The political system does not matter, as long as it supports capitalism."
--- Frank Li

Misconception 10: American capitalism is finished
Despite all the problems, America leads the world in capitalism, by leaps and bounds.

Unfortunately, American democracy has been destroying capitalism in America faster and harsher than any other forces. As a result, unless American democracy is seriously reformed soon, it will destroy capitalism in America, and hence America, as spectacularly as communism destroyed China!

Chapter 9: American Exceptionalism

"American exceptionalism" – Have you ever heard of this expression? I first heard of it more than two decades ago. Recently, it has become so problematic that I decided to write about it. To me, it is such a big, past, and troublesome expression that it has clearly contributed to the steep decline of America over the past decade, with the most prominent example being the Iraq War.

1. The definition
According to Wikipedia,

American exceptionalism is the belief that the United States is different from other countries in that it has a specific world mission to spread liberty and democracy. In this view, America's exceptionalism stems from its emergence from a revolution, becoming "the first new nation,"[1] and developing a uniquely American ideology, based on liberty, egalitarianism, individualism and populism.[citation needed] This observation can be traced to Alexis de Tocqueville, the first writer to describe the United States as "exceptional" in 1831 and 1840.[2] Historian Gordon Wood has argued, "Our beliefs in liberty, equality, constitutionalism, and the well-being of ordinary people came out of the Revolutionary era. So too did our idea that we

Americans are a special people with a special destiny to lead the world toward liberty and democracy."[3]

The term "American exceptionalism" has been in use since at least the 1920s and saw more common use after Soviet leader Joseph Stalin chastised members of the Lovestone-led faction of the American Communist Party for their heretical belief that America was independent of the Marxist laws of history "thanks to its natural resources, industrial capacity, and absence of rigid class distinctions." American Communists then started using the English translation in factional fights.[4][5]

2. America is exceptional!

America is exceptional in three aspects, at least (What is America, Anyway?):

1) America was built on a huge geographic area that was not only rich (i.e. basically un-farmed), but also replete with natural resources (e.g. coal and oil). The same thing can be said about America's two sister countries: Canada and Australia. But neither of them is close to being a beacon like America, largely because America became independent from the British much earlier.

2) America was founded on a framework that proved to be the best in the world throughout America's first 200 years (1776-1976). With freedom and justice being its core values, America developed its free enterprise system that became, and still is, the envy of the world.

3) Over the past 200 years, America has produced more great entrepreneurs than everywhere else on earth, combined! Three examples: Thomas Edison, Henry Ford, and Steve Jobs.

In short, the 20th century was clearly America's century. America, as "the shining city on a hill," was a beacon attracting many around the world to come, including me! Yes, I wanted to come to America by any means, at any cost. Luckily, I did. Happily, my American dream has come true!

3. America is not so exceptional!

America is not so exceptional in three instances, at least:

1) Domestically: American democracy is proving to be no better than the democracy practiced by the Romans and Greeks more than 2,000 years ago. As a matter of fact, democracy is failing in America today in the same way as it failed in Rome and Greece more than 2,000 years ago: debts! For more, read Chapter 7 ("Top 10 American Misconceptions about Democracy").

2) Internationally: America has proven to be no better than other nations in carrying out wars on foreign lands. A war is a war - There is little difference between imperialism (for occupation) and democratic imperialism (for spreading democracy)! Two examples:
   - Iraq: America did no better in the 21st century than the British did in the 1920s.

- Afghanistan: America has been doing no better in the 21st century than the British did in the 1850s, or the Soviets did in the 1980s.
3) Internationally and domestically: What happened over there matters here! Three examples:
    - Wars are bad! There are no real winners in any war! Read: Thomas Young, Dying Iraq War veteran, Pens 'Last Letter" to Bush, Cheney On War's 10th Anniversary.
    - Killing is bad! You can kill them in your ways over there, but they can kill you in their ways right here. Two examples: Fort Hood shooting and Boston Marathon bombings. For more, read: Senators told drone strikes cause hatred of America.
    - Truth matters! Read: Ron Paul on 9/11: Ask the right questions and face the truth.

4. Built to last

The U.S. is not exceptional at all, as compared with China and the U.K., in terms of built to last (Built to Last: Structure and Conscience).

4.1 The U.S. vs. China

America did very well for more than 200 years in her entire history. But that is "nothing" when compared with China, who mostly led the world for the first 1,800 years of its 2,013-year calendar! For more, read: America: What is China, Anyway?

4.2 The U.S. vs. the U.K.

The British Empire thrived for more than three centuries (from 16th to 18th), at least, while America is less than 240 years old.

5. Discussion

Throughout human history, great nations have risen and fallen. They rose for one and only one reason: they were exceptional for a period of time. They fell primarily for one reason as well: self-destruction!

The U.S. was exceptional for the first 200 years of its history! However, it has been falling steeply over the past decade, at least, for the same common reason: self-destruction!

How has the U.S. been self-destructing? Via both democratic imperialism and democratic socialism!

Is the U.S. really in a steep decline? Yes! Three examples:
1) High unemployment: Despite the massive government spending over the past five years, the real unemployment rate is still at about 15%! Worse yet, there is no way for it to come down in the foreseeable future, given our projected GDP growth rate at 2% per year. In other words, get used to this new norm!
2) Monumental national debt: Our national date has sky-rocketed from $9T in 2009 to almost $17T today, rising rapidly. Worse yet, nobody knows how we are ever going to pay back this debt!
3) International standing: The recent photo below shows a good example: President Obama was unable to attend APEC 2013 because of the government shutdown at home (Chapter 24: "U.S. Government Shutdown"), sending John Kerry over there, instead. Where is Mr. Kerry standing in the photo? He is "sidelined" on the right corner under the red arrow!

6. Closing

America is deeply in trouble! For more, read my book: Saving America, Chinese Style. Meanwhile, shelf this notion of "American exceptionalism," because today it does America more harm than good!

"The budget should be balanced, the Treasury should be refilled, public debt should be reduced, the arrogance of officialdom should be tempered and controlled, and the assistance to foreign lands should be curtailed lest Rome become bankrupt. People must again learn to work, instead of living on public assistance."
--- Cicero, 55BC

Chapter 10: U.S. Immigration

Immigration has always been a big deal in America (e.g. Not Legal Not Leaving). The pending Immigration Bill in Congress is said to be the biggest and most important legislation to be passed this year. However, I have already warned it as a final draw for America in Chapter 6 ("The Coming Demise of America").

In this chapter, I will express my view of U.S. immigration, holistically.

1. Putin's rumored speech

Rumor has it that Russian President Vladimir Putin addressed the Duma, the Russian Parliament, recently, and gave a speech about the tensions with minorities in Russia. Here it is:

> *In Russia live Russians. Any minority, from anywhere, if it wants to live in Russia, to work and eat in Russia, should speak Russian, and should respect the Russian laws. If they prefer Sharia Law, then we advise them to go to those places where that's the state law. Russia does not need minorities. Minorities need Russia, and we will not grant them special privileges, or try to change our laws to fit their desires, no matter how loud they*

yell 'discrimination'. We better learn from the suicides of America, England, Holland and France, if we are to survive as a nation. The Russian customs and traditions are not compatible with the lack of culture or the primitive ways of most minorities. When this honorable legislative body thinks of creating new laws, it should have in mind the national interest first, observing that the minorities are not Russians.

No, the above event never happened! Apparently it's a variation of a speech by Australian finance minister Peter Costello in 2006. It has been shopped on the Internet ever since and attributed to any world leader conveniently.

Here is my point though: do you agree with "Putin's speech"?

2. Worldviews of immigration

I have lived in several countries in three continents, including China (23 years), Japan (three years), Belgium (three years), and the U.S. (25 years). I must say that "Putin's speech" is widely accepted and practiced in all the countries in which I have lived, except for the U.S.

Why is the U.S. so different? Here is a key reason: The U.S. is a much younger country than China, Japan, and Belgium!

A key question, then, is when will the U.S. be old enough to "conform" to the "international" standard?

My answer is "now"!

3. We are all immigrants

It is a widely accepted fact that human species started in Africa many million years ago, and then we spread to the rest of the earth. Three points:
1) We found a place to live and we called it a "home".
2) We formed a community for our homes, and we called it a "country".
3) After some Europeans were fed up with their own countries, they sailed across the Atlantic Ocean, found a piece of "new" land, occupied it, and named it their own country, which is now known as the "United States of America".

4. We need our own country

The world is too big and too uneven. So we need to live in a good country, with a good government that works for the best of its citizens.

When a country is young, it welcomes many immigrants. After a country becomes old, it has more strict limits on immigration. This is commonsense and common practice throughout human history, except for the U.S. today!

5. Is America old enough?

Yes, the U.S. is old enough to have more strict limits on immigration!

Simply put: legal immigration - Yes! Illegal immigration - No!

6. Why is the U.S. so different on immigration?

Because there is no governing, but only election, in the U.S.! American politicians work for one purpose only: getting re-elected *ad nauseam*, even if it means destroying America by emptying her public treasury!

Immigration is no different from other matters of any political concern: if it helps me in my election/re-election, yes! Otherwise, no! Rule of law? Forget it! Conscious - What conscious?

Bottom line: for American politicians, everything is a game of politics, including immigration.

Game on and hell to the country! The Democrats need the Immigration Bill to seal their "rule" of America permanently. The RINOs like John McCain need it for their own personal gain (i.e. getting re-elected again)! The GOP can pass it at its own peril!

7. Closing
Once again, legal immigration - Yes! Illegal immigration - No!

Still wondering why America is so deeply in trouble? Wonder not! It's The Political System, Stupid! Immigration is just yet another aspect to reflect American government's non-functionality. For more, read my book: Saving America, Chinese Style!

Part 3: Correctly Assessing American Presidents

Chapter 11: Barack Obama vs. Harry Truman
Chapter 12: Barack Obama vs. Richard Nixon
Chapter 13: Barack Obama vs. Abraham Lincoln
Chapter 14: Correctly Assessing Chinese Leaders and
           American Presidents

Chapter 11: Barack Obama vs. Harry Truman

This chapter was triggered by this news story: Obama signs law giving himself, Bush lifetime Secret Service guard. Here is an excerpt:

> *President Barack Obama on Thursday signed into a law a measure giving him, George W. Bush and future former presidents and their spouses lifetime Secret Service protection, the White House announced.*

It immediately reminded me of President Harry Truman. What a stark contrast! Let's compare President Obama with President Truman to see how much times have really changed for America ...

1. Harry Truman

Harry Truman was a decent President overall. Here is a story, widely circulated on the Internet, about President Harry Truman:

> Harry Truman was a different kind of President. He probably made as many important decisions regarding our nation's history as any President

preceding him. However, a measure of his greatness may rest on what he did after he left the White House.

The only asset he had when he died was the house he lived in, which was in Independence, Missouri. His wife had inherited the house from her parents and other than their years in the White House, they lived their entire lives there.

When he retired from office in 1952, his income was a U.S. Army pension reported to have been $13,507.72 a year. Congress, noting that he was paying for his stamps and personally licking them, granted him an 'allowance' and, later, a retroactive pension of $25,000 per year.

After President Eisenhower was inaugurated, Harry and Bess drove home to Missouri by themselves. There was no Secret Service following them.

When offered corporate positions at large salaries, he declined, stating, "You don't want me. You want the office of the President, and that doesn't belong to me. It belongs to the American people and it's not for sale." Even later, on May 6, 1971, when Congress was preparing to award him the Medal of Honor on his 87th birthday, he refused to accept it, writing, "I don't consider that I have done anything which should be the reason for any award, Congressional or otherwise." As President, he paid for all of his own travel expenses and food.

2. Barack Obama

Here are three recent news stories about President Obama's extravagance:
1) So Who Pays for Obama's Chicago Barber to Allegedly Fly Bi-Monthly to the White House? 'It's Not Important,' He says.
2) Michelle Obama accused of spending $10m in public money on her vacations.
3) NRA hits Obama over 'hypocrisy' of armed guards for daughters.

Is President Obama a king? No! But he surely lives like one!

3. Discussion

The American Presidency may be, statistically speaking, the most dangerous job on earth, with four out of 44 Presidents being assassinated on the job (What Are the Chances of a U.S. President Being Assassinated On the Job?). Although none has been assassinated after leaving office, everything should be done to protect the Presidents, both in and out of office.

But do not confuse protection with extravagance! Three points:
1) Is today more dangerous than President Truman's time? Maybe, but it should not be! President Truman oversaw three wars: WWII, the Korean

War, and the Cold War; all of them were wars of necessity! Arguably, President Obama may deserve the credit for ending the war in Iraq, but he prolonged the war in Afghanistan for his personal and political gains! For more, read: <u>For Obama the Road to Reelection Runs through Kabul</u>.

2) The world should have been much more peaceful after the Cold War ended in 1989, but we, America, have made it more dangerous than ever, thanks to America's totally misguided foreign policy after 1989! For more, read: <u>U.S. Middle East Policy: What's Wrong?</u>

3) Is President Obama's time more economically stressed than President Truman's time? Yes! We are practically still in the Great Recession and our national debt is fast approaching $17T! So it's time for belt-tightening, right? No, not for President Obama, apparently! Leadership - What leadership?

4. Harry Truman, again

Three <u>quotes from Harry Truman</u>:

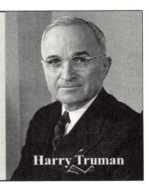

"My choice early in life was either to be a piano player in a whorehouse or a politician. And to tell the truth, there's hardly any difference."

"I never did give anybody hell. I just told the truth and they thought it was hell."

"A bureaucrat is a Democrat who holds some office that a Republican wants."

Harry Truman

Now, apply them to this (<u>Fact check on Obama's State of the Union address</u>) and see whether they make sense …

5. Closing

What a huge difference between President Truman and President Obama in life style as well as in substance!

Just like raising the tax rate on the top 1% was a bad symbolic move (as it does not solve any of the real problems at all), this life-time protection of former Presidents at taxpayers' expense is yet another bad symbolic move!

A bad symbol here, and a bad symbol there, soon we have a bad trend! No wonder America is so deeply in trouble …

Chapter 12: Barack Obama vs. Richard Nixon

This chapter was triggered by the photo below and the stories surrounding it: killing Osama Bin Laden has been hailed as one of the greatest achievements of the Obama Presidency. My immediate reaction was: what a big deal – anyone could have done it, had he (or she) been sitting in President Obama's chair!

More profoundly, it started me thinking about a much bigger question: how much lower can the bar for measuring the greatness of an American President go? Puzzled? Let me make the point by comparing President Obama with President Nixon.

1. **Richard Nixon**
According to Wikipedia,

Richard Milhous Nixon (January 9, 1913 – April 22, 1994) was the 37th President of the United States, serving from 1969 to 1974, when he became the only president to resign the office. Nixon had previously served as a Republican U.S. representative and senator from California and as the 36th Vice President of the United States from 1953 to 1961.

Nixon was born in Yorba Linda, California. He graduated from Whittier College in 1934 and Duke University School of Law in 1937, returning to California to practice law. He and his wife, Pat Nixon, moved to Washington to work for the federal government in 1942. He subsequently served in the United States Navy during World War II. Nixon was elected in California to the House of Representatives in 1946 and to the Senate in 1950. His pursuit of the Alger Hiss case established his reputation as a leading anti-communist, and elevated him to national prominence. He was the running mate of Dwight D. Eisenhower, the Republican Party presidential nominee in the 1952 election. Nixon served for eight years as vice president. He waged an unsuccessful presidential campaign in 1960, narrowly losing to John F. Kennedy, and lost a race for Governor of California in 1962. In 1968, he ran again for the presidency and was elected.

2. **President Nixon's two biggest achievements**
Personally, I think President Nixon should be considered one of the greatest American Presidents in

[recent] history (<u>Top-10 American Misconceptions about 10 Recent American Presidents</u>), perhaps even ahead of President Reagan, except for the Watergate scandal and Nixon's subsequent resignation. A bit shocked by this bold assessment? Hear me out ...

President Nixon did two extraordinary things that fundamentally changed America (and the world) for the better:
1) He established diplomatic relations with China, which was really the beginning of the end of the Cold War.
2) He created the <u>petrodollar</u> by convincing the Saudis (and hence the OPEC) to price and sell their oil in the US$ (in exchange for the U.S. military protection of the kingdom).

Next, let me briefly elaborate these two achievements.

2.1 U.S.-China relations

China had serious internal problems prior to and throughout the Nixon Presidency (<u>America: What is China, Anyway?</u>). But Nixon saw something very valuable in China: the enemy of my enemy is my friend.

At that time, the #1 enemy of the U.S. was unquestionably the Soviet Union. To end the Vietnam War and to ultimately win the Cold War, the U.S. needed China. President Nixon not only saw it (what a great visionary!), but also made it happen (what a great rainmaker!).

Here are two net results:
1) China opened up and joined forces with the U.S. against the Soviet Union.

2) China developed. The June 4, 1989 event in China (Tiananmen Square) had a direct impact on the fall of the Berlin Wall, despite the fact that it has not been adequately acknowledged in the West, yet.

2.2 Petrodollar

2.2.1 The Definition
According to Wikipedia,

A **petrodollar** is a United States dollar earned by a country through the sale of its petroleum to another country.[1] The term was coined in 1973 by Georgetown University economics professor, Ibrahim Oweiss, who recognized the need for a term that could describe the dollar received by petroleum exporting countries (OPEC) in exchange for oil.

The term *petrodollar* should not be confused with *petrocurrency* which refers to the actual national currency of each petroleum exporting country.

In addition to the United States petrodollar, a petrodollar can also refer to the Canadian dollar in transactions that involve the sale of Canadian oil to other nations.

2.2.2 Two huge benefits for the U.S.
1) The U.S. can "buy" oil by printing the US$.
2) All other countries must earn the US$ to buy oil.

2.2.3 Three questions for you
1) Can you possibly imagine a better deal for America than this?
2) Do you know this is a key reason behind America's prosperity over the past four decades?
3) Do you also know this is about to end if we stay the course?

3. President Obama's big achievements

I just can't think of any, especially when compared with President Nixon! Can you?

Maybe here are some possibilities in your mind:
1) Taxing the rich while knowing (or pretending not to know) that there are simply not enough rich out there to be taxed, even at 100%, in order to make a dent in our totally out-of-control annual deficit and monumental national debt!
2) Raising the minimum wage while the market wage is going down. Yes, we are practically still in the Great Recession, with the real unemployment rate at around 15%!
3) Gay marriage.
4) Women in combat.
5) Clean energy.

Are you serious? Oh, what about Obamacare? Good luck with that guess!

4. Discussion

Leadership matters! Experience matters! The American Presidency matters!

Elect a good President, America benefits; elect a bad one, America suffers. Unfortunately for America, we have had several very bad Presidents recently (American Presidents: Three Best and Three Worst). Why and how? It's the political system, stupid! In other words, unless the political system is fundamentally changed for the better, the streak of bad American Presidents will continue ...

Now, who will end the petrodollar? China! How? Read: Solution II for America: Term-Limits and More! Here is an excerpt:

> *By 2020, we will have printed so much money that few major economies will buy U.S. treasury bills any more. We may have to (1) accept RMB from China in order to sell them some Boeing 787s and (2) use RMB to buy goods from China. As a result, everything in Wal-Mart will be 10 times more expensive!*

In other words, China's RMB is well on its way to becoming an alternative reserve currency to the US$. Moreover, several nations (e.g. Russia and Venezuela) have already been trading with China in RMB. The trade certainly includes oil, which is really the beginning of the end of the domination of the petrodollar.

5. Closing

History is often the best judge for a big subject like a good or bad American President. With this chapter highlighting President Nixon's extraordinary achievements, do you have a better regard for him now than you did 10 minutes ago? I hope so!

I compared President Obama with President Truman in Chapter 11 ("Barack Obama vs. Harry Truman"). Now, with this comparison of President Obama vs. President Nixon, it should be very obvious to you, a reasonably intelligent American presumably, that times have really changed for America, for the worse, at the very top ...

Chapter 13: Barack Obama vs. Abraham Lincoln

After comparing President Obama with President Truman (Chapter 11: "Barack Obama vs. Harry Truman") and President Nixon (Chapter 12: "Barack Obama vs. Richard Nixon"), it's time for me to compare him with President Lincoln for two main reasons:
1) It's a well-known fact that President Obama likes to compare himself with President Lincoln.
2) Our country needs to be saved again (Saving America, Chinese Style), perhaps as badly as President Lincoln faced in his time.
   - Persistent high unemployment.
   - Monumental national debt.

1. Abraham Lincoln
According to Wikipedia,

> **Abraham Lincoln** ◀?/ˈeɪbrəhæm ˈlɪŋkən/ (February 12, 1809 – April 15, 1865) was the 16th President of the United States, serving from March 1861 until his assassination in April 1865. Lincoln led the United States through its greatest constitutional, military, and moral crisis—the American Civil War—preserving the Union,

abolishing slavery, strengthening the national government and modernizing the economy. Reared in a poor family on the western frontier, Lincoln was self-educated, and became a country lawyer, a Whig Party leader, Illinois state legislator during the 1830s, and a one-term member of the United States House of Representatives during the 1840s. He promoted rapid modernization of the economy through banks, railroads and tariffs to encourage the building of factories; he opposed the war with Mexico in 1846.

2. President Lincoln's two major achievements
1) Preserving the Union.
2) Abolishing slavery.

3. What is President Obama's major achievement?
If you ask President Obama this question, his answer is perhaps "Obamacare".

Let me answer this question by comparing what President Obama did against President Lincoln's two major achievements, one by one.

3.1 Preserving the Union
Barack Obama faced formidable challenges (e.g. the Iraq War and the Great Recession) when he was elected to the American Presidency. He did everything possible to remain popular, in order to be re-elected again. Specifically,
1) The Iraq War: he ended it – good job!
2) The War in Afghanistan: he prolonged it through a massive escalation in 2011, at least partially, for the sake of his re-election in 2012. For more, read: For Obama the Road to Reelection Runs through Kabul.

3) The Great Recession: President Obama has been dealing with it with massive government spending. As a result, our national debt has bloated from $9T in 2009 to $17T today, rapidly rising. Worst yet, nobody knows how we are ever going to pay back this debt! Worse still, we are practically still in the Great Recession, with the real unemployment rate at round 15%.

Worst of all, President Obama has proven to be incapable of crossing the party line throughout his presidency, so far. By leading only a half of the country, President Barack has actually been tearing the Union apart!

3.2 Abolishing slavery

President Obama has been the leader of the Democracy Party, the party of new slavery! Let me repeat (from Chapter 5: "The Democratic Party is the Party"):

1) The U.S. population receiving food stamps jumped from 28 million in 2008 to more than 46 million in 2012, a net increase of more than 18 million over President Obama's first term!
2) Work without pay, a new form of slavery, is an insidious form of human deprivation!

4. Obamacare

Here is an excerpt from Chapter 24 ("U.S. Government Shutdown"):

The real benefits of Obamacare for America are debatable. As far as I know, here are what's wrong with it:

1) The implementation for business has been delayed for one year, but the implementation for individuals has not been delayed. What kind of law is that?
2) Congress has been exempted from it. What kind of law is that? Congress must pass no law that does not apply to itself!
3) Obamacare includes an item which allows members of Congress to send their kids to college for free (to them). What kind of law is that?

5. Discussion

Barack Obama is no Abraham Lincoln! Look at the image below - Do you see any resemblance between the two?

Here are the two starkest contrasts between them:
1) Preserving the Union: President Lincoln did it, while President Obama has been doing the exact opposite: tearing it apart!
2) Slavery: President Lincoln abolished slavery (i.e. work without pay), while President Obama has been doing the exact opposite: he has led many into new slavery (i.e. pay without work)!

6. Closing

President Obama still has three years to shape his place in history, but I am not optimistic ...

Chapter 14: Correctly Assessing Chinese Leaders and American Presidents

On July 3, 2013, former Chinese President Jiang Zemin hosted Henry Kissinger in Shanghai. During that meeting, Dr. Kissinger reportedly commented on the five most recent Chinese leaders, one sentence for each (Kissinger commented on Five Chinese Leaders). Although Dr. Kissinger's view is widely known (Kissinger's Offers Wise Words on China), nothing has been so succinct and concise so far. So I translated his comments from Chinese (as I read it) into English for you, my fellow Americans, to appreciate.

Taking this opportunity, I'd like to comment on the 10 most recent American Presidents, one sentence for each, in the same spirit as Dr. Kissinger's, presumably …

Here is the line-up for the five most recent Chinese leaders:

Here are Dr. Kissinger's comments (my translation):
1) Mao: His charm overwhelmed everything.
2) Deng: He was one of the greatest human beings in the 20th century.
3) Jiang: Gentle and energetic.
4) Hu: Thoughtful and courteous.
5) Xi: A powerful leader!

I largely agree with Dr. Kissinger's comments, except that he was much too easy on Mao but not generous enough to Deng, whom I called, in my book (Saving America, Chinese Style), "one of the greatest peaceful transformational leaders in human history!"

Now, allow me to comment on the 10 most recent American Presidents …

1) JFK: The worst President, ever, so far, for allowing public-sector workers to unionize against the United States of America, although most Americans have yet to realize the magnitude of the damage caused by JFK. For more, read Chapter 23 ("Detroit, Public-Sector Unions, and JFK").

2) LBJ: A socialist who led America more deeply into socialism, following FDR.
3) Nixon: Could have been the best American President in the 20th century, except for the Watergate scandal and his subsequent resignation. For more, read Chapter 12 ("Barack Obama vs. Richard Nixon").
4) Ford: A decent man who served as a slot-filler.
5) Carter: Often considered the worst President in the 20th century, until more Americans come to the realization that JFK was actually much worse.
6) Reagan: Overall, the best President in the 20th century!
7) Bush I: A misguided, but decent President.
8) Clinton: The luckiest President in American history until Barack Obama! For more, read: The Myth of The Bill Clinton Presidency.
9) Bush II: The worst President, ever, until more Americans come to the realization that JFK was even worse!
10) Obama: A clueless President who knows everything about campaigning but nothing about governing, with the potential to be the worst President, ever!

Here is the race to the bottom:

What do you think? For more, jump to Part 6 ("The Race to the Bottom").

Very importantly, correctly assessing the most recent leaders of both the U.S. and China is not just an exercise for fun, but has serious undertones for both countries in terms of self-understanding, self-healing, and learning from each other ...

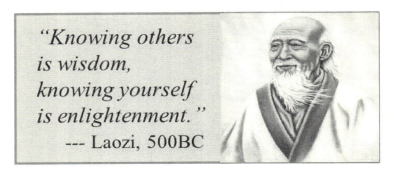

"Knowing others is wisdom, knowing yourself is enlightenment."
--- Laozi, 500BC

Now, here is the real theme of this chapter for America:
1) Unfortunately for America, American Presidents have been getting progressively worse as an overall trend! For example, Carter was thought to be the worst until Bush II surpassed him. Bush II was the worst until Obama surpassed him. Let me repeat: *"unless our political system is fundamentally changed for the better (as I suggested), the streak of bad Presidents will continue".*
2) Fortunately for America, there were a few bright lights (e.g. Nixon and Reagan), allowing America to survive. We need another bright light soon, but the prospects are dim, unfortunately (again). For more, go back to Chapter 6 ("The Coming Demise of America").

Finally, I'd like to recommend two videos to you, in order to draw a stark contrast between China and the U.S. today:

1) Eric X. Li: a tale of two political systems. Have you ever seen more confidence from China than this?
2) Obama: false hope, false messiah. Does this make sense to you?

Wake up, America!

Part 4: My Four Open Letters

Chapter 15: The First 2013 Open Letter to President Obama
Chapter 16: An Open Letter to Governor Nikki Haley
Chapter 17: An Open Letter to Senator Rand Paul
Chapter 18: My Exchanges with Senator Rand Paul

"The pen can be mightier than the sword."
--- Edward Bulwer-Lytton

Chapter 15: The First 2013 Open Letter to President Obama

(Initially published at GEI on 1/4/2013)

Dear President Obama,

Happy New Year! I hope this is the first open letter to you in 2013, thus capturing your special attention.

Congratulations on your re-election! As a staunch supporter of Mitt Romney, I was disappointed at the election result: Romney failed to win. But was I surprised by this outcome? No, not at all! As a matter of fact, in my open letter to Mitt Romney dated 5/18/2012, not only did I predict this outcome, I also spelled out a guaranteed path to success for Romney. Unfortunately, he did not listen.

How could I have guaranteed Romney such a success? Two reasons:
1) I believe I have the most accurate diagnosis for America, as well as the best solution.
2) I believe Americans will buy my diagnosis and solution if enough people will listen, especially after an endorsement by the President, who is willing to put his support behind it for the sake of America.

Because you are the President for the next four years, let me try to convince you now.

1. Summary of your first term

Overall, my assessment of your first term is well documented in [my open letter to President Obama](#) dated 6/22/2012. Here, let me highlight one issue: Obamacare, your signature achievement in your first term.

The merits of Obamacare are debatable, but the timing and the manner in which it was passed in Congress are not. Specifically,
1) Timing: It was passed when we, as a country, could least afford it. We were in the middle of the Great Recession, when a lot more basic and urgent matters should have held your attention. But they didn't. As a result, the Great Recession did much more damage to America than it would otherwise, and continuing …
2) Manner: It was passed without a single GOP vote, thus dooming your Presidency in essence and in history, despite the fact that you have just been re-elected! Why? Because an American President is supposed to be representing America, the entire country, not just half of it, along the party line!

2. Your re-election

You deserved some celebration for a few days! However, do not be carried away by your re-election victory! President George W. Bush was re-elected too! He did it by turning off the beacon to launch [the Iraq war](#) in 2003, while you did it by spending like there is no tomorrow, with a net increase of our national debt of $7T over your first term!

Both you and President George W. Bush are proven disasters for America! However, here is a key difference between you and him: he is a part of history, a very bad one (American Presidents: Three Best and Three Worst), but you can still shape your own place in history!

3. How should your re-election be viewed, really?

Domestically, it's simple: Most of the "blue" states that you won happen to be the most fiscally troubled states (e.g. California and Illinois). They will be in bankruptcy soon, like many European countries (e.g. Greece and Spain), dragging down America with them!

Internationally, read this: Hungarian-born Billionaire makes anti-socialism case in TV ad. Now, watch this short video.

4. Outlook for your second term

It does not look good for America. For example, right now, you seem to be obsessed with raising the tax rate for the top 2%, and you just got it. But it was wrong for two reasons, at least, as follows:
1) It does address the root cause, which is totally out-of-control government spending! The top 2% already pay more than 50% of the taxes. So is it really "fair" for America to take more of their money to buy more votes for the Democratic Party?
2) There will be far fewer successful Americans like Steve Jobs, Bill Gates, and even Warren Buffett, in the future.

Here are two pertinent quotes:

"The U.S. electorate has become like Pavlov's dog, salivating at the election bell and the continued promise of more treats from the treasury."
--- Jon Stimpson

"In a country well governed, poverty is something to be ashamed of. In a country badly governed, wealth is something to be ashamed of."
--- Confucius, 500 BC

Most importantly, start governing and stop campaigning!

If you stay the course, here are two predictions:
1) You will surely surpass President George W. Bush in the race of who is worse in history. For more, read: <u>American Presidents: Three Best and Three Worst</u>.
2) In less than 20 years, Americans will have this debate: Who is the worst American President ever: John Kennedy or Barack Obama? For more, read: <u>Top-10 American Misconceptions about 10 Recent American Presidents</u>.

The image below shows the big picture:

History is cruel! It has obviously been very cruel to President George W. Bush. It will be even crueler to President Kennedy 20 years from now, as Americans finally realize the magnitude of the damage he caused by allowing public-sector unions in 1961. Bad news for you!

Here is the good news for you: you can be truly great by changing the course, now! You have both the power and time to do so! All what you need is some enlightening ...

5. Enlightening President Obama

Accept my diagnosis and solution for America!

Specifically,
1) You admit that you served, throughout your first-term, for one supreme purpose only: getting re-elected *ad nauseam*, with everything else being secondary, including the long-term well-being of America. No, an American President's personal interest of getting re-elected is often not America's interest. Any doubt? Look at President George W. Bush: He was re-elected, but America tanked!

However, do not blame yourself too much. Instead, read: America: It's The Political System, Stupid!
2) You will fix the system as follows:
- Limiting the American Presidency to one-term (e.g. six years).
- Raising the statutory requirements for the American Presidency, such as the minimum age to 55 and only after having served as a state governor for one full-term, at least.
- Introducing strict term-limits for Congress, preferably one-term of six years as well.

For more, read my book: Saving America, Chinese Style.

6. Why should you heed sound advice like this?
To save America and to be truly great for yourself!

Now, let me reason with you: What's the point of your continuously staying on the left? There is no more election for you! So why don't you come to the middle and strive to be truly great in history? That way, you will not be compared with Presidents George W. Bush or Kennedy in the race to the bottom. On the contrary, you may truly become one of the greatest American Presidents, ever!

Now, imagine this: On your 55th birthday (on August 4, 2016), people will compare you with President George Washington as follows:
1) What did President Washington do? He created the republic!
2) What did President Obama do? He saved the republic!

How much greater than this do you think a human being can possibly be?

7. Is this too late for you?
No, not at all! Two examples:
1) Winston Churchill was drunk half of the time, but he led the British to victory in WWII. Today, he is widely regarded as one of the greatest British prime ministers, ever!
2) Deng Xiaoping was a bloody communist before becoming "one of the greatest peaceful transformational leaders in human history" (read: Romney vs. Deng).

Two examples of from bad to great

History is brutally honest! Shouldn't you live for America as well as for history from now on, instead of just for the Democratic Party?

8. Am I too naïve?
No, I do not think so! Many readers may think I am naïve to write you such a letter. Why? Because they are even more cynical about you now than they were four

years ago! But I remain as open-minded today as I was four years ago: again, I will give you one year before giving up on you, just like what I did with you in your first term (An Open Letter to President Obama). Three reasons:

1) As an immigrant, I dare to dream big (My American Dream Has Come True)!
2) I believe all American Presidents, including you, wanted to be great. But most just did not know how (American Presidency: Is It A Joke?). Worse yet, they became disasters in their relentless pursuit of being great (Top 10 American Misconceptions about 10 Recent American Presidents).
3) I believe in conscience (Built to Last: Structure and Conscience). If you read my diagnosis and solution, you are likely to concur. Once you concur, you will feel bad about not implementing my solution, because it would be simply unconscionable and it will stay with you badly for the rest of your life.

9. Closing

President Obama, change the course and be great, truly great! The path to greatness has already been shown to you! For the sake of America as well as for yourself, please listen and just do it!

For a complete school of thought on this, read my book: Saving America, Chinese Style.

Thank you!
--- Frank
Frank Li, Ph.D.

Chapter 16: An Open Letter to Governor Nicky Haley
(Initially published at GEI on 3/14/2013)

Dear Governor Haley,

On February 26, 2013, you made national news by saying some daring things. Here is an article about it: Nikki Haley slams Washington after meeting with Obama. Here are two excerpts:
1) When she asked Obama if he would consider a last-minute plan to shave about 2 percent from the annual federal budget without increasing taxes, the answer was "no." "My kids could go and find $83 billion out of a $4 trillion budget", Haley said. "This is not rocket science."
2) "There is something very wrong in this town."

I liked the story and promptly included it in my publication (Chapter 25: "Sequester, Capitalism, Democracy, and Money Theories"), praising you with "you are right, Governor" multiple times. It's time to balance it out by telling you that "you are wrong, Governor" in two aspects, at least:
1) Your expectation of President Obama is wrong.
2) Your expectation of Washington is wrong.

1. Your expectation of President Obama is wrong

You asked President Obama to shave about 2% from the annual budget without increasing taxes. How could you have done that? You do not seem to understand President Obama at all! Here are some facts and reasoning:

1) Barack Obama never managed a budget or payroll before becoming the President! How could you have expected him, or anybody like him, to understand, let alone to manage, a $4T budget?
2) Our national debt sky-rocketed from $9T to more than $16T during President Obama's first term. What makes you think President Obama will suddenly become a less prolific spender? He is addicted to spending, massive spending! Give him another $1T, and he will spend it in no time!
3) President Obama has successfully staged a class warfare against the rich as part of his election and re-election campaigns, winning both times. Recently, he even got the tax hikes for the top 1%. Why should he lose his appetite for more revenues, when he can't cut anything? He is addicted to spending our future and there is no limit to it!

2. Your expectation of Washington is wrong!

You said "There is something very wrong in this town". That was an understatement at best! Virtually everything in Washington is wrong today!

Why and how? Please read: It's the political system, stupid! Specifically, let me give you two reasons:

1) President Obama was too young and too inexperienced when he took office. Worse yet, he served his first term for no purpose other than "getting himself re-elected *ad nauseam*", to the extent that he even manipulated the war in

Afghanistan to his re-election advantage (read: <u>For Obama the Road to Reelection Runs through Kabul</u>)! Fortunately for America, the Presidency is limited to two terms.

2) For Congress, it's infinitely worse, because of the lack of term-limits. Most, if not all, of the members of Congress serve for no purpose other than "getting re-elected *ad nauseam*". They spend their entire incumbency trying to get themselves re-elected by any and all means, including destroying America by emptying her public treasury! Most of them are career politicians. For them, serving has never been about us or about the U.S. – It's all about them, themselves only!

In short, they all serve themselves first, their party second, their constituents a remote third, and their country dead last!

Here is the net result: "Game on and hell to the country!"

Still wondering why America is so deeply in trouble today? Wonder not! Once again, please read: <u>It's the political system, stupid</u>!

3. Closing

I believe I have the most accurate <u>diagnosis for America</u>, as well as the best <u>solution</u>. For a complete school of thought, please read my book: <u>Saving America, Chinese Style</u>!

Thank you!
--- Frank
Frank Li, Ph.D.

Chapter 17: An Open Letter to Senator Rand Paul

(Initially published at GEI on 3/21/2013)

Dear Senator Paul,

America is desperately in need of a great transformational president, and I think you are the best candidate for 2016. Here are five main reasons:
1) You are a Republican who is fiscally conservative.
2) You are not a neo-conservative, whose love for wars is just as bad for the U.S. as any liberal's love for handouts.
3) You are far better than any other possible Republican candidate. Very importantly, just say "no" to career politicians!
4) Like father, like son. Ron Paul could have been a good President, but he never got the chance. You should have a chance, and you are guaranteed to have one, if you heed my advice!
5) America does not need another Bush (e.g. Jeb) or Clinton (e.g. Hillary)! Just say "no" to any more political dynasties! Remember: we are a republic, not a monarchy! Nepotism, even by the vote of the people, has been deadly to American democracy (e.g. What's The Real Cost of The Iraq War?)!

As a staunch supporter of Mitt Romney, I was disappointed by Romney's loss in 2012. But was I surprised by it? No, not at all! As a matter of fact, in my open letter to Mitt Romney dated 5/18/2012, not only did I predict the eventual outcome, I also spelled out a virtually guaranteed path to success for Romney. Unfortunately, he did not listen …

How could I have guaranteed Romney sure success? Two reasons:
1) I believe I have the most accurate diagnosis for America, as well as the best solution.
2) I believe Americans will buy my diagnosis and solution if enough people will listen, especially after an endorsement by a presidential candidate, who is willing to put his support behind it for the sake of America.

Specifically, here is how you are guaranteed to win in 2016:
1) You must promise to be a one-term (i.e. four years) President, dedicating yourself to running the country, instead of spending the entire first term running for re-election. In other words, just do the best for the country without pandering to special interest groups!
2) You must promise to fundamentally transform America's political system by changing the Constitution as follows (Towards An Ideal Form of Government):
   - Limiting the American Presidency to one-term (e.g. six years).
   - Raising the statutory requirements for the American Presidency, such as the minimum age

to 55, and only after having served as a state governor for one full term, at least.
- Introducing strict term-limits for Congress, preferably one-term of six years as well.

Now, based on these new criteria, are you qualified to be the President? No, you are not. You will be only 54 if you become the President around January 20, 2017, and you have never served as a state governor.

This is both a challenge and an opportunity for a transformational leader!
1) You must rise to the top in the current system, or never have a chance to transform it from the top.
2) Once at the top, you make the system better by requiring your successors to be even better than you!

Any doubt? Look at Deng Xiaoping!

Deng was a bloody communist before becoming "one of the greatest peaceful transformational leaders in human history" (Romney vs. Deng)! In other words, could Deng have done it without being a [bloody] communist first? No! He would never have had the chance!

Now, imagine this: On your 59th birthday (January 7, 2022), Americans will compare you with President George Washington as follows:
1) What did President Washington do? He created the republic!
2) What did President Paul do? He saved the republic!

112

How much more do you think a human being can possibly achieve?

Senator Paul, be great, truly great! The path to greatness has already been shown to you. For the sake of America as well as for yourself, please listen and just do it!

For a complete school of thought on this, read my book: Saving America, Chinese Style. Here is an excerpt (page 4,763 of 6,468, Kindle Edition):

Thank you!
--- Frank
Frank Li, Ph.D.

Chapter 18: My Exchanges with Senator Rand Paul
(Initially published at GEI on 4/25/2013)

On March 21, 2013, I published an open letter to Senator Rand Paul (Chapter 17), urging him to run for the President in 2016. On that same day, I emailed the letter to Senator Paul's office.

Here is Senator Paul's email reply:

==

From: U.S. Senator Rand Paul <senator@paul.senate.gov>
To: frankxli@yahoo.com
Sent: Thursday, April 18, 2013 1:49 PM
Subject: Reply from Senator Rand Paul

April 18, 2013

Dear Mr. Li,

Thank you for taking the time to contact me and encouraging me to run for the office of the President of the United States of America. I am honored by your support and kind words.

As a United States Senator, I am focused on serving the Commonwealth of Kentucky in the Senate and balancing the federal budget. Rest assured that as long as

I hold office, I will work to vigorously defend the proper role of the federal government, as outlined by the Constitution.

Sincerely,

Rand Paul

Rand Paul, MD
United States Senator

===

Here is my email reply to his email reply:
===

From: Frank Li <frankxli@yahoo.com>
To: U.S. Senator Rand Paul <senator@paul.senate.gov>
Sent: Thursday, April 18, 2013 2:12 PM
Subject: Re: Reply from Senator Rand Paul

Dear Senator Paul,

Thank you very much for your reply!

However, as compared with my letter, your reply is so average. As I said in "An Open Letter to Senator Rand Paul", America is desperately in need of a great transformational leader, with concrete ideas and commitments, not someone who will just say "to vigorously defend the proper role of the federal government, as outlined by the Constitution." On top of that, the Constitution is too old - It needs to be seriously amended as I suggested (Saving America, Chinese Style).

The sooner you are committed to my suggestions (yes, one term), the more likely you are to win in 2016. Or it will be President Hillary Clinton, guaranteed!

I thank you very much for your attention and look forward to your adopting my suggestions ASAP.

Best regards,

--- Frank
Frank Li, Ph.D.
==

I will keep you posted of any further exchanges with Senator Paul ...

Part 5: Leadership

Chapter 19: Top Three Leaders: the U.S. vs. China
Chapter 20: The First Obama-Xi Summit
Chapter 21: American Presidency: Is It a Joke (II)?

Chapter 19: Top Three Leaders: the U.S. vs. China
(Initially published at GEI on 5/9/2013)

Democracy (e.g. the U.S.) vs. autocracy (e.g. China), which one is better? Well, on top of a system analysis (Towards An Ideal Form of Government), let's look at the top leaders.

As both the U.S. and China recently changed, or re-affirmed, their top leaders, there is no better time than now to compare the leaders in the two nations to draw a stark contrast.

In this chapter, I will briefly compare the top three leaders between the U.S. and China, in the executive branch only.

For the U.S., they are (from left to right):
1) Barack Obama, the American President.
2) Joe Biden, America's VP.
3) John Kerry, America's Secretary of State.

For China, they are (from left to right):
1) Xi Jinping, the Chinese President.
2) Li Yuanchao, China's VP.
3) Li Keqiang, China's Prime Minister.

The table below compares them from some basic, but important, aspects:

	The U.S.			China		
Name	Obama	Biden	Kerry	Xi	Li, Y.	Li, K.
Born (Year)	1961	1942	1943	1953	1950	1955
Starting age at current job	47	66	69	59	62	57
Previous job	Senator	Senator	Senator	VP	CPC H/R Boss	Vice Premier
Ever served as a state governor?	No	No	No	Yes	Yes	Yes

Highlights:
1) Barack Obama was too inexperienced (and too young) when he became the American President in 2009.
2) The three U.S. leaders "jumped" to their current jobs, while the three Chinese leaders "advanced" to their current jobs, well prepared, mostly as deputies for many years.
3) None of the three U.S. leaders has ever served as a state governor, while all the three Chinese leaders have.

Three notes for America:
1) Experience matters! You must have served as a state governor for one full term at least before being eligible to run for the President! For more, read: The American Presidency: Let's Redefine It, Now!

2) Age matters! Both experience and wisdom come with age. Any doubt? Read: <u>Jerry Brown, California's Grownup Governor</u>. For more, read: <u>American Presidency: Raising The Minimum Age to 55!</u>
3) Leadership matters! How could the fortuitous leaders in America possibly compete against the Chinese leaders nurtured in a GE-like way? No way, absolutely! For more, read: <u>America: What is China's Political System, Anyway?</u>

<u>Once again</u>, "in a competitive world today, all that a hiker needs to do, when chased by a hungry grizzly, is to run a bit faster than the other hiker!"

Chapter 20: The First Obama-Xi Summit
(Initially published at GEI on 6/6/2013)

The first Obama-Xi summit is about to happen (June 7-8, 2013). It should be a good thing, regardless of the expectations or outcomes, because improved understanding through dialog between the two largest economies on earth is always a good thing, not only for themselves, but also for the rest of the world.

For me, this is yet another opportunity to shed some light on U.S.-China relations. Two notes about this summit:
1) The U.S. requested the meeting. Xi agreed to stop by, in California, at the end of his trip to Latin America and Mexico.
2) There seem to be numerous issues on the table (e.g. US, China hold talks before Obama-Xi summit expected to be long on issues and short on trust). However, they are for the U.S. side only. There are few issues on the China side!

1. Xi's priorities internationally

Xi became China's President in March 2013. Since then, he has visited several countries, including Russia, Africa, and Latin America! Although schedules and convenience mattered, it showed his priorities as follows:
1) Russia was his first trip abroad as the President. For more, read: The Xi-Putin Summit, China-Russian Strategic Partnership, And The Folly of Obama's 'Asian Pivot'.
2) The U.S. was not on his short list, and then, only when the U.S. requested it!

In short, to me, here is a subtle message from China to the U.S.: you are not as important as you think you are.

Does this message make sense? Yes, a great deal of sense, to me at least! Americans should take note and here is why: The U.S. is a very consumer-friendly country, with many laws favoring consumers. However, in other parts of the world and throughout human history, it's the other way around: a creditor (e.g. often a producer) has far more power than a debtor (e.g. often a consumer)!

2. The issues on the U.S. side

Here are three big issues off the top of my head:
1) North Korea and Iran.
2) Obama to confront Chinese president over cyber-attacks on US.
3) Business deals, such as Smithfield Deal Signals China's Need for Meat, Dairy, Other Food Buys.

Simply put, all of them are self-inflicted issues. Let me explain them, one by one ...

2.1 North Korea and Iran

Here are two articles of mine from more than one year ago and they are still valid today:
1) America: What to Do with North Korea?
2) U.S. Middle East Policy: What's Wrong?

2.2 Cyber-attacks

Three fundamental questions for you:
1) Cyber-attacks: did you know that we, Americans, invented them? For example, read: Obama Ordered Sped Up Wave of Cyber-attacks Against Iran.
2) Did you know that our military spending is 50% of the world's total military spending (It's The Out-Of-Control Spending on Military, Stupid!)? Why so big? If your answer is for self-defense, you simply do not get it!
3) Cyber-attacks vs. military attacks, which one is worse? For more, read: What's The Real Cost of The Iraq War?

2.3 Business deals

We owe China about $2T. What's wrong with their trying to buy some American companies? They are not allowed to buy hi-tech companies. They are not even allowed to buy some wind farms (Obama blocks Chinese wind farms purchase near Navy base). Now, are we going to prevent them from buying a food company?

Have we really been so deeply brainwashed that we all truly believe that a debtor has more power than a creditor?

3. The issues on the China side
There are no U.S. issues on the China side, other than just staying the course with some sweet talks from time to time.

Xi said, last year (i.e. before becoming the President), something like this: "I do not want to be told by some big bellied foreigners about what to do."

President Obama is certainly not big bellied physically. What about intellectually? Remember, he is way short in experience and achievements as compared with President Xi. For more, read Chapter 19 ("Top Three Leaders: the U.S. vs. China").

4. Discussion
I have repeatedly stated, over the past five years, that "the Chinese system (i.e. capitalism + autocracy), albeit with many endemic problems of its own, appears to be slightly better than America's" (Saving America, Chinese Style).

Here is another simple example to illustrate the difference between the U.S. and China: what's the job of the President? Apparently,
1) For President Xi, it is chasing the Chinese dream.
2) For President Obama, it is chasing the next election. For more, read: Obama's Top Goal: For Dems To Win The House In 2014.

Need some concrete evidence? Last week, President Xi was in Latin America and Mexico, making huge commercial deals, for the benefit of his country, while President Obama was in Chicago, doing huge fund-raising for Democrats (Chicago braces for Obama fundraising visit), for the benefit of his party!

Once again, "In China, there is no election but only governing. In America, there is no governing but only election."

Oh, a very important international matter: Syria. Here are two news stories:
1) Russia warned not to deliver missiles to Syria.
2) Syria peace talks likely to be postponed as Russia plans to ship more weapons.

Sound like a little bit of the Cold War again? Yes, to me! Here are two key differences:
1) China is largely engaged with Russia now. Remember the Xi-Putin summit mentioned earlier?
2) The U.S. is no longer the economic monopoly it was in the past.

Why have the times changed so much? China is improving its situation while ours worsens! Here is another sharp contrast:
1) Obama effectively ends U.S.-manned space flight.
2) China's Latest Manned Space Mission to Launch This Month.

More seriously, America has been self-destroying via democratic imperialism abroad and democratic socialism at home. For more, read: Top 10 American Misconceptions about Democracy.

5. Closing
Stop self-destruction! Stop blaming others for our own problems! Stop China bashing!

To know more about China's future, read this: China's next chapter.

Chapter 21: American Presidency: Is It a Joke (II)?

(Initially published at GEI on 10/23/2013)

This chapter was triggered by this news article: Bill Clinton: Chelsea would make a great president. While I appreciate the humor behind President Bill Clinton's joke, it's time for me to re-visit the subject of American Presidency: Is It A Joke?, with this sequel ...

Here are my three key points:
1) It's time for America to amend its Constitution to make the American Presidency a more serious job.
2) America is a republic, not a monarchy!
3) America can no longer afford another Democratic President, be it a Clinton or even an Obama!

Next, let me elaborate these three points one by one.

1. Constitutional changes

In my book (Saving America, Chinese Style), I suggested the following constitutional changes to the American Presidency as absolutely necessary:

1) Limiting the American Presidency to one-term (e.g. six years).
2) Raising the statutory requirements for the American Presidency, such as the minimum age to 55 and only after having served as a state governor for one full-term, at least.

Case in point: America must raise the competency of the American Presidency via constitutional changes!

2. America is a republic, not a monarchy!

Instead of having one king or queen as in a monarchy, America now has 536 kings or queens! Here is the math: one President, 100 Senators, and 435 House Representatives. Many of them work for one purpose only: getting re-elected *ad nauseam*, even if it means destroying America by emptying her public treasury! Worse yet, many of them seek to enrich themselves. Here is a recent story from 60 Minutes: Washington's open secret: profitable PACs.

Worse still, America now has its own "royal" families: the Kennedys, the Bushes, or even the Clintons!

Case in point: Is this how America should look like? More profoundly, is this an ideal form of government? For more, read: Towards An Ideal Form of Government.

3. America can no longer afford another Democratic President!

America is being destroyed by democratic socialism (Chapter 3), championed by all the Democratic Presidents since FDR (except for Truman)! For more, read Chapter 5 ("The Democratic Party is the Party of New Slavery!").

Now, back to President Clinton … He was not even a good President - What makes him think Chelsea would make a great President? President Clinton was the luckiest American President until President Obama! For more, read: The Myth of The Bill Clinton Presidency.

For President Obama, watch this video: The Obama Presidency.

Case in point: The Democratic Party is the Party of New Slavery!
1) Another President Clinton? Just say "no"!
2) Another Democratic President? Just say "no"!

4. Closing

Leadership matters! Experience matters! The American Presidency matters!

Part 6: The Race to the Bottom

Chapter 22: Singing "The Internationale" in America?
Chapter 23: Detroit, Public-Sector Unions, and JFK
Chapter 24: U.S. Government Shutdown

Chapter 22: Singing "the Internationale" in America?

(Initially published at GEI on 1/18/2013)

Everybody growing up in the East knows the song of "The Internationale". It was very well composed both in form (e.g. rhythm) and in content (e.g. wording). Growing up in Communist China (1949-1976), I sang it almost daily and I was brainwashed to believe every word in it.

Here is a big problem though: the entire content proved to be completely wrong!

What's the point? Well, Michigan passed a Right-to-work bill in December 2012. The next day, President Obama showed up in Michigan, criticizing it.

As someone who is now very tired of hearing President Obama talking, I purposefully listened to him this time for the sake of writing this piece. Surely, the President did not disappoint me: he practically sang the song of "the Internationale" on the podium!

For this writing, I began translating "the Internationale", which I know by heart in Chinese, to English. Half way through, I got a better idea: why not trying to find something better on the Internet? I did!

Watch this video: Singing "The Internationale" in English with captions. It's a beautiful song, isn't it? The only problem is that almost every word in it is misleading and false!

Now, compare this song with President Obama's speech (Obama criticizes Michigan right to work bills): they are so similar!

In my book (Saving America, Chinese Style), I identified six similarities between democracy and communism as follows:
1) Destruction of capitalism
2) Brainwashing
3) Ideology
4) Kleptocracy
5) 'You didn't build that'
6) Stupidity.

I believe democracy, as we practice it today, leads inexorably to communism. Three notes with regard to communism and democracy:
1) By "communism", I am referring to the East, led by the former Soviet Union and seconded by Communist China (1949-1976), although the folks there call it "socialism".
2) By "democracy", I mean the West, led by the U.S.
3) Although the U.S. has been "loosely" called a democracy for more than 200 years, by the simple but strict definition of one person, one vote, the U.S. was not a democracy until 1964. For more, read Chapter 4 ("Restoring America").

Bottom line:
1) Communism collapsed in 1989, with the collapse of the Berlin Wall!
2) Democracy is now failing in the West in the same way as it failed in Rome and Greece more than 2,000 years ago: debts!
3) The Chinese system (i.e. capitalism + autocracy) appears to be slightly better than democracy, as we practice it today.

For more, read my book: <u>Saving America, Chinese Style</u>!

Wake up, America! It's time to make a U-turn! My proposal, as described in <u>Saving America, Chinese Style</u>, is the best on the table!

Big social changes can happen in two ways:
1) A violent revolution like <u>Mao</u> succeeded in China in 1949.
2) A peaceful transformation like <u>Deng</u> did in China from 1978 to his death in 1997.

America is desperately in need of a great transformational leader like China's Deng! Will that be President Obama (Chapter 15: "The First 2013 Open Letter to President Obama")? Highly unlikely, given the track record of his first term! But let's wait and see what he has to say next week in his inaugural speech for his second term. I am afraid he will again sing "<u>The Internationale</u>" on the podium, without realizing it ...

President Obama, you still have two choices for your place in history:

Either

OR

For details, read Chapter 15 ("The First 2013 Open Letter to President Obama").

Chapter 23: Detroit, Public-Sector Unions, and JFK
(Initially published at GEI on 8/8/2013)

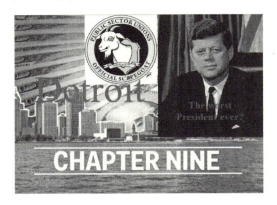

Detroit is in bankruptcy – what a disaster!

There are numerous articles about this disaster already, from diagnosis (Detroit, and the Bankruptcy of America's Social Contract), to its implication for the rest of the country (Detroit's Warning for Chicago - and Others), to a possible solution (Detroit Ran Into The Inviolable Rule Of Economics). What's missing in the mainstream media are the wisdom and honesty to identify the root cause of the Detroit disaster in order to work toward a real solution and prevent more disasters like this from happening across the country.

Here, I will try to do just that: identify the root cause of the Detroit disaster and provide a real solution!

1. The Detroit disaster

Detroit was not built in one day, nor did it go bankrupt in one day. Here are two facts highlighting the Detroit disaster:

1) Population: It declined from its peak of 1,849,000 in 1950 to 713,000 in 2010 (Demographic history of Detroit).
2) Abandoned houses today: 78,000 (Broken City: Detroit).

For more, read Decline of Detroit and Detroit's Beautiful, Horrible Decline - photos.

2. Analysis

There are two essential ways to analyze the Detroit disaster: is it due to a contingency or is it a systemic failure? If it's the former, which means non-repeating, we should identify the major problems and fix them one by one. Otherwise, it's a systemic failure, which means there are big structural problems. Obviously, for Detroit (and other liberal strongholds), it is a systemic failure. We should therefore focus on the biggest problem first. The reason behind the intense focus is that unless the biggest problem is identified and solved, little else matters. Besides, once the biggest problem is solved, some other big problems may be minimized.

Apparently, for the mainstream-media, the Detroit disaster is due to a contingency. So everybody has been looking for problems everywhere (e.g. mismanagement and corruption). But for me, it's obviously systemic. So let's focus on the biggest problem first ...

What is the biggest problem in Detroit (as well as in many other U.S. cities and states)? Crushing pension obligations for public-sector workers, both active and retired (Detroit not alone under crushing pension obligations)!

How bad is the public-sector situation in America?

1) The public sector is too big! Read this report ([Government Employees and Manufacturing Jobs: Takers and Makers](#)). Here is an excerpt: *"More Americans work for the government than work in construction, farming, fishing, manufacturing, mining, and utilities combined."*
2) Public-sector workers are overpaid! Here is an excerpt from the [same report](#): *"state and local government employees earned total compensation of $39.60 an hour, compared to $27.42 an hour for private industry workers, a difference of over 44%!"*
3) The pensions of [most] public-sector retirees are too good to be true!

Why such a big mess with the public sector? In 1961, President Kennedy allowed public-sector workers to unionize against the United States of America ([Executive Order 10988](#))!

Did not JFK know what he was doing? Yes, he did, boldly against FDR's explicit warning against it ([Letter from FDR Regarding Public-Sector Unions](#))!

Why did JFK do it anyway? He did it to specifically insure his re-election, which became moot after his assassination, but the damage was done! In other words, JFK sacrificed America's future to achieve his personal aggrandizement! More broadly, it's called "getting re-elected *ad nauseam*, even if it means destroying America by emptying her public treasury" ([Saving America, Chinese Style](#))!

The day of reckoning is here, finally!

3. Judgment

Here is an excerpt from my book (Saving America, Chinese Style):

> *President Kennedy might well be recognized as the worst American President twenty years from now, as America finally realizes the magnitude of the damage he caused by allowing public-sector unions in 1961!*

Have you yet realized the magnitude of the damage caused by JFK?

Yes, JFK is the ultimate culprit behind the Detroit disaster, with the worst for the rest of America yet to come!

In summary, not only was the problem of public-sector unions created by JFK systemic, the reason behind JFK's action (i.e. getting re-elected *ad nauseam*) was also systemic! It's time to fix both systemic problems, at once! It is existential, for both Detroit and the U.S.!

4. A real solution

Political reforms! Specifically,
1) Abolishing all public-sector unions immediately and banning them forever, with an executive order to undo President Kennedy's Executive Order 10988!
2) Setting term-limits for all the top political offices, with the American Presidency being one term (e.g. six years)!

For more, read my book: Saving America, Chinese Style!

5. Discussion

Throughout human history, great nations have risen and fallen. They rose for one and only one reason: they were exceptional for a period of time. They fell primarily for one reason as well: self-destruction!

The U.S. has long been exceptional! It has been falling steeply over the past decade, at least, for the same common reason: self-destruction!

How has the U.S. been self-destructing? Via democratic socialism, epitomized by public-sector unions (as well as democratic imperialism, epitomized by the Iraq War)!

In short, public-sector unions are totally communistic, and must therefore go!

Detroit is not an exception - Detroit's problems are common throughout the U.S.! Unless we successfully address the biggest problem in Detroit (i.e. public-sector unions), little else matters: we will not get Detroit back for real and worse yet, more U.S. cities and states will follow Detroit to bankruptcy!

More broadly, it's time for us to critically examine our country as an entitlement society! Here are five principles someone has applied to Detroit recently (widely circulated on the Internet):
1) You cannot push the poor into prosperity by pulling the rich out of prosperity!
2) For what one person receives without working, another person must work without receiving.
3) The government cannot give somebody anything that the government does not first take from somebody else.
4) You cannot multiply wealth by dividing it!
5) When half of the people get the idea that they do not have to work because the other half is going to take care of them, and when the other half gets the idea that it does no good to work because somebody else is going to get what they work for, that is the beginning of the end of any nation.

Now, compare America with Europe: Detroit is just yet another example of our Greece (Greece's Unemployed Young), with many more cities and states to follow, such as my home state Illinois like Spain and even California like Italy ...

One by one, both cities and states, democracy, as we practice it today, will drive them into bankruptcy, until all is there (America's European Past and Future)!

6. Detroit = 9/11?

I believe Detroit is a new 9/11 moment for America. The grand approach for us should be the same: either we face the truth and seize the opportunity to change for the better, or we ignore the truth and continue on a path of self-destruction!

What was the truth behind 9/11? Read: Ron Paul on 9/11: Ask the right questions and face the truth! Have we already faced the truth as a nation? No, not yet! Because of that, we have been on a path of self-destruction (e.g. the Iraq War and Patriot Act) since then!

What is the truth behind Detroit? Democracy, as we practice it today, does not work! More specifically, by allowing public-sector unions, President Kennedy committed the worst act against the United States of America, ever! Therefore, not only should we explicitly name JFK the worst American President (so far), we must also undo his act by revoking Executive Order 10988 and then fundamentally reform our political system!

More broadly, was 9/11 a terror act against America? Yes, it was! But even that was nothing when compared with what American politicians have done to America, with JFK epitomizing it! For more, read my book: Saving America, Chinese Style!

7. Closing

America is deeply in trouble. Detroit is just yet another example!

Chapter 24: U.S. Government Shutdown
(Initially published at GEI on 10/9/2013)

The U.S. government has been shut down, albeit partially, since October 1, 2013. Is it a good thing for America? No, not for the short term, as it has been causing some inconvenience to some people at least! But for the long term, it is likely to be a good thing. Here is why: The U.S. has been on a wrong track (e.g. out-of-control spending) for a long time. It's time to change the course, whatever it takes. No pain, no gain!

1. Who shut down the government?
President Obama and the Democrats!

Here is an excellent article on this subject: Who Shut Down the Government? The Democrats Or GOP? Here are some highlights:
1) Obamacare is the law of the land. No argument!
2) Our Constitution requires "spending via appropriation", giving the right of appropriation to Congress. In other words, Congress decides on what items to spend. It just happened that the House majority has decided to spend on everything but Obamacare this time. It is their constitutional right to do so. No argument!
3) The Senate majority (i.e. the Democrats) does not like it, not does President Obama. Instead, they

want a "clean" bill that funds everything, including Obamacare. When they did not get what they wanted, they shut down the government! No argument!

2. Who will re-open the government?

It should be those who shut it down in the first place! Yes, that means President Obama and the Democrats. They should "blink" first in this stare-down exercise. If that happens, our government will have actually worked this time.

On the other hand, if the House majority blinks first, it will be business as usual: America will continue on the wrong track!

3. Obamacare

The real benefits of Obamacare for America are debatable. As far as I know, here are what's wrong with it:
1) The implementation for business has been delayed for one year, but the implementation for individuals has not been delayed. What kind of law is that?
2) Congress has been exempted from it. What kind of law is that? Congress must pass no law that does not apply to itself!
3) Obamacare includes an item which allows members of Congress to send their kids to college for free (to them). What kind of law is that?

Did I get the above three points right?

4. Discussion
This shutdown highlights two problems:
1) The U.S. government no longer works in the large, regardless of the outcome of this stare-down exercise.
2) It's time to have serious political reforms, as I suggested in my book: Saving America, Chinese Style!

The debt ceiling issue is just around the corner. It will put our government in a much bigger test. Meanwhile, just remember this: it was President Obama that shutdown the government!

5. Closing
Kudos to the House majority for standing up for America this time! Will they hold on? Let's wait and see …

Part 7: America: What Are You Doing?

Chapter 25: Sequester, Capitalism, Democracy, and Money Theories
Chapter 26: Patriotism: A Seventh Similarity between Communism and Democracy
Chapter 27: America: What The Heck Is All This Political Correctness?
Chapter 28: Money and America
Chapter 29: Paul Krugman Understands Neither China Nor America!
Chapter 30: Equality in America: Oversold and Overbought!
Chapter 31: Jobs, Darn Jobs, and Steve Jobs
Chapter 32: Who Has the Best Job in America?

"Today, there are actually more communists in the U.S. than in China. Most Democrats are socialists, with the extreme left being communists!"
--- Frank Li

Chapter 25: Sequester, Capitalism, Democracy, and America
(Initially published at GEI on 2/27/2013)

A big sequester is just around the corner (A Sequester No One Wants). Worried? Do not be! It's just yet another fabricated crisis! Besides, it's only $85B, or 2.4% of the $3.6T federal budget! If we can't cut that miniscule when the budget deficit is more than $1T, how are we ever going to pay back our monumental national debt of almost $17T?

We have much bigger problems to worry about!

What are they? How about capitalism, democracy, and money theories? In this chapter, I will link them together with three stern messages as follows:
1) Capitalism is the best thing ever happened to mankind. It fed starving people and created unprecedented prosperity in the West over the past several hundred years. It is creating unprecedented prosperity in China now.
2) Democracy not only was a proven failure in human history, but also has been destroying the West over the past two decades, at least, with no end in sight.
3) America will save neither itself nor democracy by printing more money!

1. Introduction

I author a weekly column at Global Economic Intersection, which has many publications on economics. I read these publications to further my knowledge of economics. However, I have just reached a simple conclusion: most of the research as reflected in many publications is simply valueless, not unlike modern democracy, which has been faltering in the West over the past two decades, at least.

As always, I will focus on America, instead of the West.

2. America is a great country!

A simple but true statement! For more, read: What is America, Anyway?

3. Americans are innovative!

Over the past 150 years, at least, Americans invented many things that have fundamentally changed human lives for the better, from Thomas Edison's light bulb, to Henry Ford's assembly lines for cars, to Steve Jobs' i-everything.

4. Three big things not invented by Americans!

Americans did not invent these three big things:
1) Capitalism: It was invented by the Europeans. For example, Industrial Revolution started before the U.S. was founded as a country in 1776.
2) Democracy: It was practiced in Rome and Greece more than 2,000 years ago. Both failed for the same reason: debts!
3) Money theories: Many, if not most, theories of money seem to be based on one notion: Fiat money. What, then, is fiat money?

According to Wikipedia,

> **Fiat money** is money that derives its value from government regulation or law. The term **fiat currency** is used when the fiat money is used as the main currency of the country. The term derives from the Latin *fiat* ("let it be done", "it shall be").[1]
>
> Fiat money originated in 11th century China,[2] and its use became widespread during the Yuan and Ming dynasties.[3] During the 13th century, Marco Polo described the fiat money of the Yuan Dynasty in his book *The Travels of Marco Polo*.[4][5] The Nixon Shock of 1971 ended the direct convertibility of the United States dollar to gold. Since then all reserve currencies have been fiat currencies, including the U.S. dollar and the Euro.[6]

5. Money theories

There are many theories of money in existence (e.g. Quantity Theory of Money, Theories of Money, and Marx's Theory of Money). They make economics a seemingly interesting discipline. However, half of these theories can be easily eliminated by simply understanding that Quantitative Easing (or QE), a favorite policy practiced by the Federal Reserve, is just "printing money"!

Why, then, does not the Fed call QE1, QE2, etc. "printing money"? It did, for many years, until inflation it caused gave "printing money" a bad reputation! The Fed then called it "monetizing the debt", until inflation gave it an equally bad name. The latest euphemism is QE, until people suffer from the resultant inflation and hate it, as well. Any guesses for the next name for the same bad game that further erodes the U.S. dollar and causes more misery?

It's all a myth just like democracy! Artificial complexity makes manipulating large groups of people easier by keeping them uninformed, or misinformed (read: Brainwashing in Communism and in Democracy), the secret sauce of democracy, as we practice it today!

Fool me once, shame on me! Fool me twice, shame on you! Fool me three times, shame on the political system! For more, read my book: Saving America, Chinese Style!

6. The sequester
The sequester is a very minor, contrived problem, but it has certainly highlighted our true, dire situation: Our top politicians are arguing endlessly about $85B when our annual deficit is more than $1T! What's wrong with these politicians?

Here is a recent news story: Nikki Haley slams Washington after meeting with Obama. Here are two excerpts with my comments:
> 1) When she asked Obama if he would consider a last-minute plan to shave about 2 percent from the annual federal budget without increasing taxes, the answer was "no." "My kids could go and find $83 billion out of a $4 trillion budget," Haley said. "This is not rocket science."

> Yes, you are right, Governor! Anybody with reasonable intelligence could do it, except for President Obama, who does not know how to govern! Remember, Barack Obama never managed a budget or payroll before becoming the President!

2) "There is something very wrong in this town."

Yes, you are right again, Governor! Virtually everything is wrong in Washington today! Why and how? Read: It's the political system, stupid!

7. Closing
America is deeply in trouble …

Chapter 26: Patriotism: A Seventh Similarity between Communism and Democracy
(Initially published at GEI on 5/2/2013)

In my book Saving America, Chinese Style, I identified six similarities between communism and democracy as follows:
1) Destruction of capitalism
2) Brainwashing
3) Ideology
4) Kleptocracy
5) 'You didn't build that'
6) Stupidity.

In this chapter, I will identify patriotism as a seventh major similarity between communism and democracy.

1. What is patriotism?
According to Wikipedia,

> ***Patriotism*** *is a devotion to one's* country, *excluding differences caused by the dependencies of the term's meaning upon context,* geography *and* philosophy. *In a generalized sense applicable to all countries and peoples, patriotism is a devotion to one's country.*

2. My view of patriotism

Most people are patriotic by default. However, while most people love their own country by default, they do not necessarily love, or even like, their government. In other words, just because you do not like your government, it does not mean you do not love your country. Unfortunately, all too often, some people, especially many self-serving politicians, equate the love for a country to the love for its government, and *vice versa*. It was a wide-spread practice in Communist China (1949-1976), and it appears to be increasingly popular in a democracy, such as France and even America.

3. Gerard Depardieu

Here is a recent news story: Gerard Depardieu 'pleased' to become Russian Citizen. Here is an excerpt:

> *President Vladimir Putin has signed a decree granting Russian citizenship to French actor Gerard Depardieu ... Depardieu (pictured below) decided to change his citizenship following a tax reform by French President Francois Hollande, levying a 75% tax on citizens earning more than one million euros per year ... French Prime Minister Jean-Marc Ayrault called Depardieu's decision to quit France "pathetic" and "unpatriotic."*

How ironic is this story? Two points:
1) A successful French actor became a Russian citizen a little more than two decades after communism collapsed in the former Soviet Union.
2) The way he has been treated at home (i.e. France) is little different from the way communist leaders treated their citizens in the former Soviet Union or

Communist China (1949-1976), from asset confiscation to name calling of "unpatriotic"! Bad politicians use "unpatriotic" as a euphemism for "opposing my policy"!

4. Patriotism in America

I watch news on TV daily and noticed that a lot of folks coming back to America from the wars receive a hero's welcome.

On the other hand, it is my understanding that the U.S. news media is censoring itself by not broadcasting the scenes of casualty returns, such as the photo below.

While it's difficult to accept the political reason behind media "bias", I was deeply disturbed after reading the 7/22/2012 issue of Time magazine, whose cover story was "The War On Suicide". Here is an excerpt:

Every day, one U.S. soldier commits suicide. Why the military can't defeat its most insidious enemy?

Furthermore, according to the 1/28/2013 issue of Time magazine, there were 349 U.S. military suicides in 2012, more than the 295 troops killed in combat in Afghanistan during 2012.

What a total tragedy! It led to a basic question in my mind for many years: Why is America, only America, involved in so many wars on earth?

When a war and the word "patriotism" are so closely linked as in America today, it brings strong recollection of my previous life in China …

5. Patriotism in Communist China (1949-1976)
Communism means abject poverty and an absolute lack of freedom. So it's not easy to rule in communism. A powerful tool used by the rulers in Communist China was patriotism. Two examples:
1) Put up with the hardship now, as life will eventually get better. Keep hoping, as it's a patriotic thing to do!
2) Fight against the international enemies, as they all hate China (e.g. the Two Opium Wars with the British and the two Sino Japanese Wars).

Now, a personal story: one of my uncles joined the People's Volunteer Army in 1951, and was sent to Korea to "fight against the American aggressors" for a key reason: "it's better to fight them over there than here", so was the Korean War portrayed in China at that time.

Officially, he went to Korea as a patriotic duty!

Here are the two real reasons behind his going to Korea:
1) He had nothing better to do.
2) He viewed it as a way to escape poverty.

How did he fare in Korea? Well, a few days after he crossed the Yalu River, he lost one toe to frostbite during a very cold night and was immediately sent back home. Of course, he was warmly welcomed back, just as he was warmly sent off. Additionally, as a wounded war veteran, he was relatively well taken care of by the government. He passed away a few years ago at age 82.

Can you draw a little analogy between my uncle and a veteran in the U.S. today? While different people join the military for different reasons, patriotism has been a big draw, correctly or incorrectly.

6. Patriotism in America, again

Democracy, as we practice it today, means more and more poverty (e.g. Poverty In The U.S. By The Numbers) and less and less freedom (economic freedom) in America. Although neither is as bad as in Communist China yet, the worst is yet to come.

It's not easy to be a "ruler" in America – You must remain popular in order to be re-elected again and again. One effective way to do it is to keep the defense industry strong. The major downside is that the world must have conflicts and America must have enemies …

With conflicts and enemies come the excessive needs of keeping the defense industry strong and the exaggerated need of sending troops everywhere, often in the name of patriotism. As a result, since the Cold War ended in 1989, America has been busily involved in many conflicts all over the world, especially in the Middle East (U.S. Middle East Policy: What's Wrong?). Remember the picture below?

WMD was the justification America invaded Iraq in 2003, which turned out to be totally false. Here are some stats about the Iraq War: Tens of thousands of Iraqis died. What about the U.S. casualties? 4,486 deaths and over 100,000 wounded! But for what? Bush II's re-election, most likely! For more, read:
1) Hubris: The Inside Story of Spin, Scandal, and the Selling of the Iraq War.
2) Blagojevich and Pearl Harbor: They Are Related!

Another justification for the Iraq War was "it's better to fight them over there than here." The similarity to the Korean War as it was portrayed in China is obvious.

Oh, do you know someone who went to the Iraq War? If yes, what was his/her official reason? Was it patriotism, like my uncle's?
1) If yes, then America's brainwashing machine has actually worked better than Communist China's propaganda machine.
2) If no, have you found out the real reasons yet? If not, maybe in a few years. Meanwhile, read: Dumb and Dumber – The U.S. Army lowers recruitment standards ... again.

Now, what about The Afghan War: Read: For Obama the Road to Reelection Runs through Kabul. Here is an excerpt:

> *The real goals of the Afghanistan escalation are domestic and electoral ... The real purpose of these 300,000 soldiers is to make Obama look tough as he heads toward the next US presidential election.*

While the reality is debatable, the perception alone is frightening! Michael Hastings's article (The Runaway General) further confirms the perception. Worse yet, it is patently obvious that the troop withdrawal plan was timed perfectly for President Obama's re-election schedule. Apparently, no price was too high for Americans to pay for President Obama's re-election!

Here is a must-read article: Thomas Young, Dying Iraq War veteran, Pens 'Last Letter" to Bush, Cheney On War's 10th Anniversary. Here is an excerpt:

> *I write this letter, my last letter, to you, Mr. Bush and Mr. Cheney. I write not because I think you grasp the terrible human and moral consequences of your lies, manipulation and thirst for wealth and power. I write this letter because, before my own death, I want to make it clear that I, and hundreds of thousands of my fellow veterans, along with millions of my fellow citizens, along with hundreds of millions more in Iraq and the Middle East, know fully who you are and what you have done. You may evade justice but in our eyes you are each guilty of egregious war crimes, of plunder and, finally, of murder, including the*

murder of thousands of young Americans—my fellow veterans—whose future you stole.

7. Discussion

Here are two quotes:

1) Winston Churchill: "One day President Roosevelt told me that he was asking publicly for suggestions about what the war should be called. I said at once 'The Unnecessary War'."
2) Sun Tzu: "All war is deception."

Here is a simple but succinct criterion to judge the validity of a war: If you are not willing to go yourself or send your child there, the war is not worthwhile! With this criterion, ask yourself this question: after WWII, which war with American involvement was worthwhile?

Okay, I know what you are thinking: 9/11. Here is a must-read article: Ron Paul on 9/11: Ask the right questions and face the truth.

Yes, America has been the major source of instability around the world since 1989, when the Cold War ended!

No, the U.S. military is not (supposed to be) a global 911 service. But it has been, thanks to the war hawks in the U.S. political-military complex.

Yes, America has been trying to save the world, while bankrupting itself at home. Read this recent story: Afghanistan Manufacturing the American Legacy. Here is an excerpt:

A decade ago, playing music could get you maimed in Afghanistan. Today, a youth ensemble is traveling to the Kennedy Center and Carnegie Hall. And it even includes girls.

Is it progress in Afghanistan? Yes! Should we Americans pay for it? No! Is this a justification, in any way, shape, or form, for the decade-long war in Afghanistan? A bloody "no"!

Now, a piece of advice from a gun-enthusiastic friend of mine: "watch out, the military that is 'patriotically' protecting us now may one day turn against us. So keep the guns!"

Need more reasons to keep the guns? Read this: Why Is Obama's Growing DHS Army Buying Armored Vehicles?

8. Closing

America is a great country and Americans are a great people. But it's the political system, stupid! More specifically, it's getting re-elected *ad nauseam*, stupid! So whenever an American politician utters the word "patriotism", be it for a war or a tax hike, watch out! To me, it sounds eerily like a communist talking when I was growing up in China …

"Patriotism is supporting your country all the time, and your government when it deserves it."
--- Mark Twain

Chapter 27: America: What The Heck Is All This Political Correctness?

(Initially published at GEI on 6/20/2013)

For my business as well as for fun, I publish twice a week:

1) Wednesday serious: It's my weekly column at Global Economic Intersection. I make special efforts to write well on various subjects, from business to politics.
2) Friday funny: It is often a tasteful joke contributed by a reader. This is no longer much work for me: just select one from the numerous submissions and email it out.

Occasionally, the Friday funny is also a platform for me to collect some ideas to write about, which, on a day in September 2012, was political correctness, or PC.

1. The joke

Here is my joke back on a day in September 2012:

1) Old Chinese proverb: "give a man a fish, you feed him for a day. Teach a man to fish, you feed him for a lifetime."
2) New American proverb: "give a man a welfare check, a cell phone, cash for his clunker, food stamps, section 8 housing, Medicaid, 100 weeks of

unemployment checks, a 40-ounce malt liquor, needles, drugs, contraceptives, and designer Air Jordan sneakers, he will vote Democrats for a lifetime."

2. The responses

Here are the three responses I received that day:
1) "This would be funnier if it wasn't true!"
2) "Sounds like a winning strategy to me, unfortunately."
3) "I'm surprised that a guy with your intelligence would pass along such inane and racist statements."

Why so different in responses to the same joke? Here is my response:
1) It's true, although it may not be funny to some!
2) Racist? No! Politically incorrect? Yes!

What, then, is political correctness?

3. Definition: political correctness

According to Wikipedia,

> **Political correctness** (adjectivally, **politically correct**; both forms commonly abbreviated to **PC**) is a term which denotes language, ideas, policies, and behavior seen as seeking to minimize social and institutional offense in occupational, gender, racial, cultural, sexual orientation, certain other religions, beliefs or ideologies, disability, and age-related contexts, and, as purported by the term, doing so to an excessive extent. In current usage, the term is primarily pejorative,[1][2] while the term **politically *in*correct** has been used as an implicitly positive self-description. Examples of the latter

include the conservative *The Politically Incorrect Guide* published by Regnery Publishing and the television talk show *Politically Incorrect*. In these cases, the term *politically incorrect* connotes language, ideas, and behavior unconstrained by a perceived orthodoxy or by concerns about offending or expressing bias regarding various groups of people.

4. Discussion

In a previous post (Solution II for America: Term-Limits and More!), I stated: *"democracy is a luxury we, as a country, can no longer afford"*. In other words, democracy must be changed, at least, to have a chance to survive.

One of the first areas of change is PC. Here is why:
1) PC emboldens falsehoods from the very top (American Democracy: Massive Falsehoods at The Top!) to the bottom (Arizona Sheriff Joe Arpaio to Appeal Judge's Finding His Department Engaged in Racing Profiling).
2) PC has cost us dearly. For example, profiling is a common scheme used in CSI and at Israeli airports, but we pretend it's not necessary and we don't allow it in our airport screening, resulting in massive inconvenience to tens of thousands of people on daily basis! As a matter of fact, every time I am at the airport, I can't help but think Osama Bin Laden might have actually won the terror war against America …

PC may have cost me a bit too … My book (Saving America, Chinese Style) is politically incorrectly titled!

Need some proof? Here is a conversation I had with a friend recently:

Frank: I just published a book.
Friend: Good! What's the title?
Frank: Saving America, Chinese Style.
Friend: I like the first part, but not the second.
Frank: Will you read it?
Friend: No!
Frank: Why not?
Friend: You want to make us like China?

Now, add your own examples and thoughts on PC …

5. Closing

We have gone way too far on PV! Undo some of the changes and restore some commonsense!

Here is a must-watch video on PC: Dr. Benjamin Carson Addresses National Prayer Breakfast, Criticizes Obamacare!

Chapter 28: Money and America
(Initially published at GEI on 7/18/2013)

America is not only a beautiful country, but also a great country!

One key reason behind America's greatness, as compared with her two sister countries Canada and Australia, is because America became independent from the British much earlier (What is America, Anyway?).

Unfortunately for America, there appears to be a severe drawback attached to this earlier independence: forgetting, if not a total loss of, history (America's European Past and Future)! For example, America, the current super-power on earth, is repeating the same mistake made by her predecessor, the Great Britain, with regard to [fiat] money, reserve currency, and the economy ...

1. Fiat money

Most currencies today are fiat money, including the U.S. dollar, the British Pound Sterling, and China's RMB. According to Wikipedia:

> ***Fiat money*** is money that derives its value from government regulation or law. The term ***fiat***

currency is used when the fiat money is used as the main currency of the country. The term derives from the Latin fiat ("let it be done", "it shall be").[1]

Fiat money originated in 11th century China,[2] and its use became widespread during the Yuan and Ming dynasties.[3] During the 13th century, Marco Polo described the fiat money of the Yuan Dynasty in his book The Travels of Marco Polo.[4][5] The Nixon Shock of 1971 ended the direct convertibility of the United States dollar to gold. Since then all reserve currencies have been fiat currencies, including the U.S. dollar and the Euro.[6]

2. Reserve currency

Here is a description of reserve currency, according to Wikipedia:

*A **reserve currency**, or **anchor currency**, is a currency that is held in significant quantities by many governments and institutions as part of their foreign exchange reserves. This permits the issuing country to purchase the commodities at a marginally lower rate than other nations, which must exchange their currencies with each purchase and pay a transaction cost. For major currencies, this transaction cost is negligible with respect to the price of the commodity.*

3. Money and economy

Fiat money was invented by the Chinese more than 1,000 years ago, for the purpose of "printing money as the government sees appropriate." Since then, it has been used, misused, and abused by many governments around the world.

A reserve currency (or "RC") is earned! Typically, the currency of the country with the strongest economy on earth earns the honor of being the "dominant" RC. Currently, the dominant RC is the U.S. dollar (for less than 100 years so far). Before that, it was the British Pound Sterling (for about 200 years). What is the key behind an RC? Confidence and trust!

Any government can print its own money, any time and in any quantity. When the currency is not an RC (e.g. Ethiopian birr), the impact is limited: domestically of course, as well as to the country's trading partners. But when the currency is a dominant RC like the U.S. dollar today, the impact of massive money printing is world-wide and huge, with one net result: a loss of confidence and trust in that currency as the dominant RC!

Historically, when a dominant RC is being massively and "irresponsibly" (viewed internationally) printed, it signals the beginning of the end of that currency as a dominant RC. This was what happened to the British Pound Sterling (How the British Pound Sterling Fell from Grace), and this is just what's happening to the U.S. dollar!

Which currency, then, has been challenging the U.S. dollar? China's RMB! Here are two pertinent facts:
1) China has already been trading with several nations (e.g. Russia, Venezuela, and several Asian nations) in RMB. Additionally, China recently reached currency agreements with several western countries, including the U.K (U.K., China Reaches Currency Deal), Japan (Currency Agreement for Japan and China), and Australia (Australia, China reach agreement on currency deal).

2) It's widely recognized that China's RMB is on the way to becoming a major alternative RC to the U.S. dollar. Here is a recent article: <u>Is the Yuan About to Replace the Dollar as the World's Reserve Currency?</u> Here is an excerpt:

> *A country's rise to economic dominance tends to be accompanied by its currency becoming a reference point, with other currencies tracking it implicitly or explicitly. For a sample comprising emerging market economies, we show that in the last two years, the renminbi (RMB) has increasingly become a reference currency which we define as one which exhibits a high degree of co-movement (CMC) with other currencies. In East Asia, there is already a RMB bloc, because the RMB has become the dominant reference currency, eclipsing the dollar, which is a historic development.*

Now, is China's RMB perfect? No, not at all! China has its own challenges (e.g. <u>China Accounts For Nearly Half Of Worlds New Money Supply</u>). However, the trend is undeniably here: China is well on her way to becoming the #1 economy on earth by 2030, and its RMB will inevitably become a major RC!

4. Money and America

The U.S. dollar is losing its status as the dominant RC! What does that mean to America? Our standard of living will plummet, because we can no longer massively import (yes, America has trade deficits with more than 90 countries) by simply printing more money!

Specifically, <u>petrodollar</u> no more - What a pity!

The U.S. dollar is losing its status as the dominant RC for two main reasons: China's rise and America's self-destruction, just as I elaborated in my book (Saving America, Chinese Style) as the reasons behind America's decline.

How has America been self-destructing? Here is a simple equation Americans must understand about our monetary policy and our economy:

> QE = massive money printing
> = massive monetizing of debt
> = massive use of steroids

Three notes about America's prosperity (at least in the past):
1) It has come from the real strength of our economy, not the massive use of steroids!
2) It has come from the real leadership at the top, such as the creation of the petrodollar by President Nixon (Chapter 12: "Barack Obama vs. Richard Nixon").
3) It has come from capitalism (Chapter 8: "Top 10 American Misconceptions about Capitalism"), not

democracy, as we practice it today (Chapter 7: "Top 10 American Misconceptions about Democracy").

Unfortunately for America, all of these "magic" ingredients seem to be gone and elusive today! How can things become so bad? <u>It's The Political System, Stupid!</u> Here is a concrete example: Senator Obama voted against raising the debt ceiling to $9T in 2006, which he labeled "unpatriotic". But under President Obama, our national debt has ballooned to almost $17T, rising rapidly!

Simply put, QE (Quantitative Easing) is not only irresponsible and additive, but also suicidal! Domestically, it does not solve our real problems (e.g. unemployment). Internationally, it signals the beginning of the end of the U.S. dollar as the dominant RC, and hence the beginning of the end of America, as we know it.

Now, is high unemployment a real domestic problem the Fed has been trying to solve? Yes! Apparently, the scope of the Fed's job has recently been expanded to explicitly targeting to lower the unemployment rate to 6.5%. What a tragedy! Two points:
1) Unemployment should not be the Fed's job explicitly!
2) The target of 6.5% is possibly obtainable only through the reduction of the participation rate, thanks to our severely flawed method of calculating the unemployment rate. With the economy growing at around 2% a year in the foreseeable future, we are not even able to accommodate the population growth!

In short, the real unemployment rate will remain high (i.e. above 15%), despite trillions of dollars out of the EQs (QE1, QE2, and QE3)!

Oh yes, Wall Street has been doing very well, thanks to the Fed ...

5. Closing

We must change our course, if we are to leave a viable country to our children! For more, read my book: <u>Saving America, Chinese Style</u>!

Chapter 29: Paul Krugman Understands Neither China Nor America!
(Initially published at GEI on 7/25/2013)

When Paul Krugman writes, people read. Here is a recent publication by Professor Krugman: Hitting China's Wall. It has caused strong reactions not only in the U.S., but also in China (Hitting China's Wall – The Chinese version). Hesitantly, I decided to respond to Professor Krugman, holistically!

Why the hesitation? Because I am not an economist (thankfully so)! Although I have published extensively on a variety of subjects, including money (e.g. Chapter 28: "Money and America"), I am uncomfortable debating an economist in his terms (e.g. stats and darn stats).

Why responding this time? Because I care deeply about U.S.-China relations! When Professor Krugman writes inappropriately about China like that, I am determined that "he is not going to get away with it without hearing from me"! Very importantly, I actually have published my opinion about Professor Krugman several times already. So this response is just a further extension to my previous criticism of him, making it more complete.

Why holistically? You can't understand Professor Krugman without touching Keynesian economics!

1. Paul Krugman does not understand China!

Here is an excerpt from a previous article of mine (America: What is China, Anyway?):

> *Unfortunately, the American political-media complex in general has not been forthright about China, thanks to "brainwashing"! Moreover, many China "experts" in the West focus too much on the technical details, without adequately understanding China (e.g. the essence of its political system and the culture).*

Professor Krugman epitomizes my statement! His understanding of China is very limited, and at least partially erroneous! Worse yet, because we, as human beings, tend to see things from our own perspectives, how could Professor Krugman possibly understand a remote land as China when he does not even understand America, his home?

2. Paul Krugman does not understand America!

Here is an excerpt from an earlier publication of mine (Karl Marx and John Keynes):

> *Worse yet for America, despite the fact that both Presidents Hoover and FDR admitted that it was WWII, not the massive government spending, that finally got America out of the Great Depression, many left-wing extremists (e.g. **Paul Krugman** and Robert Reich) still try to keep this biggest lie of the 20th century going by actively advocating deficit spending as the only way out of today's Great Recession. These folks have made their livings out*

of Keynesian economics. They blindly, irresponsibly, and shamelessly promote it, just like communists promoted Marxism a few decades ago, even in the face of mounting evidence that what they sell does not work, nor has it ever actually worked.

Oh, **Paul Krugman** *appears to possess great credibility after winning a Nobel Prize. Mikhail Gorbachev also won a Nobel Prize! But I called Gorbachev "brainless and reckless" for the way he dismantled the Soviet Union. I have the same regard for* **Paul Krugman** *for the way he has been damaging America's economy, through relentless promotion of Keynesian economics!*

3. "Hitting China's Wall"

Now that I have asserted my position, let me specifically focus on Professor Krugman's recent article: Hitting China's Wall ...

3.1 "It's harder to figure out what's really happening in China"

Here is how Professor Krugman begins his article:

> *All economic data are best viewed as a peculiarly boring genre of science fiction, but Chinese data are even more fictional than most. Add a secretive government, a controlled press, and the sheer size of the country, and it's harder to figure out what's really happening in China than it is in any other major economy.*

While his argument is basically true in a very gross sense, it points out how little he knows about the essentials of the subject he is opining about, but that didn't seem to deter his offering an opinion! Surely he is not presenting a way to understand China, economy-wise or otherwise! A good way to understand China is to read my book (Saving America, Chinese Style)! It comprehensively explains to my fellow Americans what America is and what China is, in terms of history, socialism, communism, capitalism, and democracy!

Without that basic knowledge, most Americans do not even understand America, let alone China!

Here are two key points about China:
1) China's political system: it could be simply called a "dictatorship without a dictator." Their system, albeit with many endemic problems of its own, appears to be slightly better than America's political system.
2) China's economic system: It's state capitalism. Overall, today's Chinese government is more pro-business than today's American government in many ways, even per Steve Wynn! Note that

capitalism is not perfect. But today, bad capitalism in China is often better than good socialism in the U.S.!

These two key points put China solidly on the right track, with everything else being secondary! Yes, they are the key reasons behind China's rise and America's fall over the past two decades, at least, with no end in sight!

With that, here are three salient points about China:
1) Do not be distracted by the unimportant details! For example, China's GDP grew 7% last quarter. Fine! Oh, no, it was only 6.5%. Fine, too! It's the direction that is important, not a particular number! Note that in a mostly top-down economy like China's, low-level people forge numbers to please the boss! Yes, China's stats are often even less trustworthy than our own doctored numbers!
2) Do not think the Chinese are wrong simply because they are different.
3) Treat most things in China like Chinese food: enjoy it, but do not go into the kitchen to see how it's made!

3.2 "Yet the signs are now unmistakable: China is in big trouble"

Here's Professor Krugman's pesky opinion about something he admittedly knows nothing about: China is in big trouble. Perhaps yes. But they admit it and they are addressing their issues! America is also in big trouble. But we deny it even while allowing it to worsen!

3.3 "What keeps China's consumption so low?"

They save too much! We Americans spend too much! However, saving too much is better than spending too much, especially since their exports are so high while developing their own domestic consumption model, vs. Americans, who spend too much money and import too much, resulting in our national debt being $17T and growing rapidly!

3.4 "It's running out of surplus peasants"

A complete disregard for the obvious truth! With 1.3B people, the Chinese government's overwhelming concern has always been jobs, not a shortage of laborers! A great project in China is massive urbanization: trying to move some 300M peasants into cities in the coming decade, which will dramatically uplift their quality of life and consumption (e.g. gas for cooking and hot water for showers). For more, read: [Premier Li Keqiang Wants More Chinese in the Cities](#).

Now, the [Arthur Lewis](#) point ... Professor Krugman refers to it extensively in his article. The [Arthur Lewis](#) point looks correct, but Professor Krugman's application is not. In response, I will devote Section 4 "The [Bob Costas](#) point" to it.

3.5 "We were afraid of the Chinese. Now we're afraid for them"

My fellow Americans, do not worry about China (or anybody else). Look to ourselves first!

Everything in China is well under control! For example, in an explosive growth economy like China's over the past three decades, there are inevitably many bubbles (e.g. real estate). However, the Chinese government, with their control, can choose which bubble to burst and even when!

The system over there works, albeit with many problems of its own, unlike our political system here, which does not work!

The world would have been a much better place, if we Americans would only have minded our own business. Two facts:
1) Our military spending in more than the next 16 biggest spending countries combined. Yes, America has been the source of instability around the world since the Cold War ended in 1989.
2) America has been trying to save the world, while bankrupting itself at home!

4. The Bob Costas point

Bob Costas is perhaps one of the best known sportscasters in the U.S. A fixture of Olympics broadcasting, Mr. Costas has openly and obviously grown up on China over the past two decades. For example,
1) In the 1996 Olympics (Atlanta), he was so nasty and shamelessly biased against Chinese athletes that the Chinese-American community strongly protested it.

2) Mr. Costas became more and more balanced through the 2000 Olympics (Sydney) and the 2004 Olympics (Athens). He became a Chinese angel in the 2008 Olympics (Beijing), and remained a Chinese angel through the 2012 Olympics (London).

Here is the Bob Costas point: Mr. Costas did China bashing in 1996 for three reasons:
1) He did not understand China very well.
2) He did it to please his main audience, without realizing that he had severely offended the Chinese-American community, in addition to doing a huge disservice to his main audience.
3) He thought he could get away with his China bashing, unpunished.

Professor Krugman did his China bashing, albeit much more mildly than Mr. Costas did in 1996, for the same three reasons, I suspect. Too bad, he caught my attention this time (and maybe others as well).

Hopefully Professor Krugman will have a Bob Costa epiphany: you just can't ignorantly and irresponsibly attack China like that, even in America, as Bob Costas did in 1996, without meeting heavy rebuttal from those who are better informed!

5. Closing

Professor Krugman should study the works of economists who are real China experts. For example, Michael Pettis has been living, teaching, and consulting in China for well over a decade. For a couple of years, Professor Pettis has said that the rebalancing of China's economy would reduce China's GDP to about 3% on average over the next decade. However, according to Professor Pettis, China is not headed for disaster.

Given the trouble at home, Professor Krugman would do a more useful service if he concentrated on the U.S. economy, going beyond Keynesian economics, of course!

Finally, allow me to repeat this simple observation: "China is quickly becoming yesterday's America, while America is quickly becoming yesterday's China." What does that mean? Remain uninformed or you can read my book: Saving America, Chinese Style!

Chapter 30: Equality in America: Oversold and Overbought!
(Initially published at GEI on 8/29/2013)

Yesterday (August 28, 2013) was a big day in America. It was the 50th anniversary of Dr. Martin Luther King Jr.'s famous "I have a dream" speech, and President Obama spoke from the same spot in front of Lincoln Memorial where Dr. King stood and delivered that speech exactly 50 years ago.

I watched this anniversary event with mixed emotions ... On one hand, I think Dr. King was a great American, and that speech was one of the best speeches ever. On the other hand, I think equality, one of Dr. King's messages, has been oversold and overbought in America in several major ways, just like American Dreams (American Dreams: Over Sold and Over Bought!), another one of Dr. King's messages.

Puzzled? Hear me out ...

1. Martin Luther King Jr. and America
I have deep respect for Dr. King for the following reasons:
1) He pursued an undeniable worthwhile cause and ultimately paid the ultimate price for doing so.
2) His message of equality is irrefutable.

3) His additional message of non-violence is particularly important today, not only for America, but also for the rest of the world (Chapter 2: "Democratic Imperialism").

However, it's premature to call Dr. King a "founding father", as Time magazine did recently (8/26-9/2 issue, as shown below) for one key reason: America, as a country, is more deeply in trouble than ever (Chapter 6: "The Coming Demise of America"). Until a real solution is found, all the past should be open for scrutiny, including JFK's legacy (Chapter 23: "Detroit, Public-Sector Unions, and JFK") as well as the Civil Rights movement, epitomized by the final realization of one person, one vote. For example, how could you have one person, one vote, without requiring a voter ID? More on this later ...

Many believe Dr. King's "I have a dream" speech was one of the best speeches ever recorded in human history. However, speech is speech, reality is reality. With regard to various American Dreams, here are three of my earlier publications:
1) American Dreams vs. America.
2) My American Dream Has Come True.
3) American Dreams: Oversold and Overbought!

Now, let's focus on equality ...

2. Equality

There should be only two types of equality in America: equal justice and equal opportunity.

Not equal outcome or equal pay!

We must accept the following inequalities as the reality they are:
1) We are born unequal! Some even argue that more than 50% of our ability, physical as well as mental, is determined by genes, I agree with this argument. The older (and hopefully wiser) I become, the more I agree with this argument, empirically at least!
2) Race matters! For example, it is widely acknowledged that while the Asians excel academically, they are hopeless in many sports (e.g. track and field). For more, read: Swimming, Olympics, and More.
3) Sex matters! Men and women are different! For example, men are typically physically stronger than women and are hence more suitable for "tough" jobs such as manual labor and combat.

4) Culture matters! A friend of mine serves as a volunteer at a food distribution center, providing food for the hungry. Never has he met an Asian there!

5) Environment matters! By "environment," I mean such things as family (e.g. two parents vs. single parent), school, your friends, and even the country you live in.

Because of these inequalities, some human beings will be more successful than others, as it must be, unless you prefer communism, wherein everyone shares equal misery!

3. The system matters more than anything else!

Communism achieves absolute equality by pulling everybody down, dirt poor – Yes, everyone has the same: nothing! [Been there, done that](#)!

Capitalism has proven to be the only system for prosperity. In a capitalistic society, you are allowed to achieve your full potential, which often means that you can live a life far better than others, if you are willing to work for it (and if you are good and lucky). In other words, capitalism allows you to achieve maximal inequality, in your favor. Better yet, the rising tide lifts all boats!

Democracy, as we practice it today, looks more and more like communism! In pure democracy (i.e. <u>one person, one vote</u>), people are treated absolutely equally in an election, without any difference between a parasite (e.g. <u>Obama is going to pay for my gas and mortgage</u>) and a genius like Bill Gates: one vote!

4. A few words on China and America

The biggest professed champion of equality I have encountered in my life was Chairman Mao. The image below shows one example.

"*Women hold up half the sky.*"
--- Mao Zedong

Unfortunately, most of Mao's teachings turned out to be blatant, self-serving lies! Sounds familiar? Think about the campaign promises in the U.S.!

With <u>one person, one vote</u> becoming a reality as a result of the Civil Rights movement, America was fundamentally changed from a republic with full-blown capitalism and a limited-version of democracy to full-blown democracy and an increasingly crippled version of capitalism, totally against the wisdom of the founding fathers (Chapter 4: "Restoring America")!

Still wondering why America is so deeply in trouble today? Wonder not! It's democracy, as we practice it today, stupid! For more, read my book: Saving America, Chinese Style!

5. Discussion

As the "Land of Opportunity", Americans must value equal opportunity. Unfortunately, our present version of equality is equal outcome. It is completely unworkable and destructive, just as we are experiencing today!

A recent analysis showed that a family in Hawaii living entirely on public assistance had the equivalent standard of living as a family with a bread winner earning $30/hour. However, the average wage for that actual bread winner in Hawaii is only $20/hour. Where's the equality when someone living off others is 50% better off than the ones actually working?

For more, read: It pays not to work: Hawaii residents receive highest welfare benefits in the U.S.

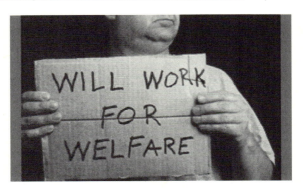

6. Closing

Equality is a good concept in general. However, as in everything else, the devil is in the details. In America, equality has been oversold and overbought, in my humble opinion …

Mildly speaking, Dr. King's "I have a dream" speech may have been misinterpreted (Was MLK's 'I Have a Dream' Speech Misinterpreted?).

More profoundly, it's time for America to fundamentally question democracy like the Chinese do! Watch this video (again): Eric X. Li: a tale of two political systems.

Chapter 31: Jobs, Darn Jobs, and Steve Jobs
(Initially published at GEI on 9/5/2013)

Labor Day just passed by. Let's focus on jobs. Here are my three succinct positions:
1) Jobs: High unemployment is merely a symptom, not a root cause.
2) Darn jobs: The more we try to fix the symptom, without addressing the root cause, the worse the symptom will become, overall.
3) Steve Jobs: It is the entrepreneurs like Steve Jobs that have made America truly great, by creating not only millions of real jobs, but also some brand new industries.

1. Jobs
How bad is the jobs situation in America today? Here is a good article: Will the Real Unemployment Rate Please Stand Up? The real unemployment rate is around 15%.

Want to read more? Here are two interesting articles:
1) The Real Unemployment Rate Is Worse Than You Think.
2) Temporary jobs becoming a permanent fixture in US.

2. Darn jobs

Most, if not all, American politicians worry about their own jobs only, nothing else, such as Americans' jobs. Because of that, they keep trying to fix the so called "jobs problem," a symptom, without even attempting to identify the root cause. Since, as in all politics, the appearance is more important for election/re-election than the reality, the easiest way for them to appear to address the jobs problem is to keep throwing money at it. After all, it's not their money, anyway! Three examples:

1) <u>Unemployment Isn't the Fed's Only Job</u>. Yes, even the Federal Reserve has been targeting the unemployment rate to lower it to 6.5%. With the economy growing at around 2% per year for the foreseeable future, we are not even able to accommodate the population growth (which has a lot to do with illegal immigration). As a result, the only way to achieve 6.5% is via the reduction of the participation rate. The Fed is surely aware of that, but is pretending not to know, even as millions of Americans have left the job market in frustration! In short, the Fed serves the politicians, not America, in this particular instance, at least!

2) <u>U.S. Cuts Take Increasing Toll on Job Growth</u>. In this article, the authors cry: *"The number of federal workers forced to work shorter hours soared this summer — to 199,000 in July, from 55,000 a year earlier — in a sign of the problems that <u>federal budget</u> policy is causing for the economy."* For these authors, no cut of any government expense should practically be done, in the name of job creation or job preservation, if nothing else! They are intoxicated in a happy family syndrome: you pretend to be working, while the government pretends to be paying you, all at taxpayers' expenses, though – but who cares!
3) <u>What We Need Now: A National Economic Strategy For Better Jobs</u>. The only thing correct in the entire article by Professor Reich is the title! Yes, we need more, and better, (full-time) jobs for those Americans still willing to work. However, the only real strategy to create a lot of good jobs for the long haul is to restore manufacturing, which requires a more pro-business environment (e.g. less regulations and less unions), which requires political reforms! In other words, we must restore the U.S. as a republic with full-blown capitalism and a limited version of affordable democracy (Chapter 6: "The Coming Demise of America")!

Bottom line: Capitalism is the key to prosperity and, yes, jobs. Democracy, as we practice it today, is a luxury America can no longer afford!

Here is a talking point argument endlessly repeated by many liberals: because more than 60% of America's economy is supported by consumers, businesses should hire as many employees as they can and pay them as well as they can, because employees are consumers after all. The economy will improve with increased consumption.

What a communistic idea based on circular reasoning! According to [Wikipedia](),

> **Circular reasoning** *(also known as **paradoxical thinking** or **circular logic**), is a [logical fallacy]() in which "the reasoner begins with what he or she is trying to end up with". The individual components of a circular argument will sometimes be logically [valid]() because if the premises are true, the conclusion must be true, and will not lack relevance. Circular logic cannot prove a conclusion because, if the conclusion is doubted, the premise which leads to it will also be doubted.*

What the liberals fail to understand, or refuse to acknowledge, is that [most] businesses are not charities. Business is to make money, making it existential to control costs, including employee expenses. Unfortunately, the current American administration is working furiously in the wrong direction, adding huge new costs such as various regulations, Obamascare, and extended unemployment benefits to businesses.

Very importantly, having consumers who are incapable of paying bills is worse than having no consumers! Any doubt? Just look at the recent U.S. meltdown due to subprime mortgages! Buyers who do not pay must be avoided at all costs!

Americans must understand that, without major political reforms as I suggested, the best days for America are gone, for good! Anybody who tells you otherwise is dreaming or simply lying!

Here are two outcomes for America, really:
1) 30% will fail to thrive, while 70% will be successful like they were in the 1990s. This is the best outcome we can hope for and will be possible only if we reform our political system as I suggested in my book ("Saving America, Chinese Style").
2) 100% will be poor. This will undoubtedly occur if we stay the course.

3. Steve Jobs

America has been great largely because it has been the "Land of Opportunity", allowing folks like Steve Jobs and many other self-made men (Part 8: "America: A Nation of Self-Made Men") to be great!

These great individuals are uniquely American, as America has produced more of them over the past 200 years than everywhere else on earth, combined! They worked hard, obtained fantastic results, and were richly and fairly rewarded (Chapter 8: "Top 10 American Misconceptions about Capitalism")! They created not only millions of real jobs, but even some brand new industries, leaving America's competitors in our dust ...

Unfortunately for America, these American giants are now being demonized as the top 1%, all the while America is being converted from the "Land of Opportunity" to the "Land of Entitlement" ...

Capitalism supports democracy! Promote democracy by destroying capitalism? You will end up having neither!

4. Closing

America was not built in one day, nor will it go down in one day!

America has been declining steeply for the past decade, at least, with no end in sight! High unemployment is merely a symptom. Unless we identify the root case, there will be no real solution!

What's the root cause? Democracy, as we practice it today! It kills capitalism, jobs, and ultimately America!

What's the real solution? Restoring America, via political reforms, to be a republic with full-blown capitalism and a limited version of affordable democracy! For more, read my book: <u>Saving America, Chinese Style</u>!

Chapter 32: Who Has the Best Job in America?
(Initially published at GEI on 9/25/2013)

My answer is Pat Sajak, the host of ABC's "The Wheel of Fortune"!

As a matter of fact, my wife and I like this show enough that we often watch it through our dinner. It is fun for everybody involved, including the host and hostess, the game participants, and the viewers. Here are two main reasons why it's fun:
1) It is simple and reasonably intelligent.
2) It hands out good stuff only (e.g. cash and exotic trips).

At the end of the show, I often sigh to my wife: "I wish I could have Pat's job."

Wouldn't it be nice if we all could have Pat's job? It's easy, it's well paid, and it has good job security.

Now, do you realize that many of our politicians (e.g. members of Congress) can match with Pat in job appeal?

Here's how:
1) It's easy: Keep handing out good stuff to make some people happy (in exchange for their votes), despite the fact that our national debt is fast approaching $17T!
2) It's well paid, by any standards, for a public servant. They get full retirement benefits and lifetime healthcare for just six years in office! Better yet, under Obamacare, their children get to attend college for free (to them) - All at our expense for doing such a great job that our country is broke.
3) It has good job security, especially when driven by "getting re-elected *ad nauseam*," using the huge advantages an incumbent has over any challengers.

There is, however, a big difference between Pat's job and our top politicians' job: a for-profit company pays the former, while taxpayers foot the bills for the latter. When the politicians work for no purpose but their own re-election, nobody is looking after the country, especially its fiscal side! Congress spends and spends like there is no tomorrow! No wonder our national debt is almost $17T already, rapidly rising ...

Ever heard of Congressman John Dingell (pictured below)? According to Wikipedia:

> ***John David Dingell, Jr.*** *(born July 8, 1926) is an American Democratic politician who has been a member of the United States House of Representatives continuously since entering Congress on December 13, 1955. On June 7, 2013 he reached 20,997 days of membership, surpassing Robert Byrd as the longest-serving member of Congress in history.[1] Dingell is a long-time member and former Chairman of the House Energy and Commerce Committee.*

On June 2, 2013, Mr. Dingell was interviewed by ABC's George Stephanopoulos for soon to be the longest serving member of Congress. When asked among the more than 25,000 votes he cast, what was the most important one he remembers, Mr. Dingell answered: "the Civil Rights act in 1964!" What an accomplishment! Here is an excerpt from Chapter 30 ("Equality in America: Oversold and Overbought!"):

> *With one person, one vote becoming a reality as a result of the Civil Rights movement, America was fundamentally changed from a republic with full-*

blown capitalism and a limited-version of democracy to full-blown democracy and an increasingly crippled version of capitalism, totally against the wisdom of the founding fathers!

I don't know much about Mr. Dingell, so I have no personal opinion about him. However, it's a well-known fact that Congress has an abysmal <u>disapproval rate of 87% among Americans</u>! Two questions:
1) Would you be proud like Mr. Dingell to have long "served" in an institution like our Congress, which, with his complicity, is providing great personal success to him while destroying the greatest economy the world has ever known?
2) Why is Congress so overwhelmingly disapproved by American people?

<u>It's The Political System, Stupid!</u> Specifically, it's the career politicians like John Dingell, Nancy Pelosi, Harry Reid, John McCain, and Lindsey Graham that are the problem for America: they are self-serving politicians and they work for one purpose only: getting re-elected *ad nauseam*, even if it means destroying America from the extreme right (Chapter 2: "Democratic Imperialism") and the extreme left (Chapter 3: "Democratic Socialism"). For more, read Chapter 6 ("The Coming Demise of America").

Now, let me repeat (from Chapter 3: "Democratic Socialism"):

"Both career politicians and career welfare recipients are parasites. Together, we have been destroying America from inside out!"

--- Frank Li

Part 8: America: A Nation of Self-made Men!

Chapter 33: Self-Made Men
Chapter 34: Walter Young: A Self-Made Man!
Chapter 35: Jon Stimpson: A Self Made Man!
Chapter 36: Fred Herrmann: A Self-Made Man!
Chapter 37: Pin Ni: "His Own Warren Buffett"

"The answer is work; the question is why."
--- Anonymous

Chapter 33: Self-Made Men

I believe I have the most accurate diagnosis for America, as well as the best solution. To best appreciate them, we must know, or re-learn, who we are as a nation!

Among the many definitions of America, I like this one the best: "we are a nation of self-made men"!

The notion of self-made men was perhaps popularized by Frederick Douglass in an article published in 1872 (Self-Made Men). Since then, there have been numerous publications on self-made men. Two examples:
1) Abraham Lincoln: Self-Made Man.
2) 25 of the Greatest Self-Made Men in American History.

I will write about four self-made men whom I personally know very well. Two notes:
1) All of them are successful businessmen. They worked hard for their success and now are fully enjoying it.

2) None of them would have been so successful without being in America. They all love America dearly!

The first man is Walter Young.

Walter is a 91-year-old senior citizen, currently active as the CEO of Emery Winslow Scale Company, headquartered in Seymour, Connecticut.

Walter noticed me in 2009, when I led the scale industry to fight against an anti-competitive regulation called VCAP (Verified Capability Assessment Program). He and I have been good friends since then. As a matter of fact, Walter is a father figure to me (and he is actually two years older than my late father), and we chat about everything, from business to politics, without any constraints. For example, I have been constantly advising him: "retire today and find something better to do, such as reading and writing". But he has yet to listen …

These three men will follow Walter:
1) Jon Stimpson, Owner and President, National Scale Technology (Huntsville, AL).
2) Fred Herrmann, Owner and President, Indiana Scale (Terre Haute, IN).
3) Pin Ni, President of Wanxiang America (Elgin, IL).

They are all strong supporters of my business, as well as my endeavor as a writer. I have learned a lot from them, so will you.

Chapter 34: Walter Young: A Self-Made Man!

Walter Young is the owner and CEO of Emery Winslow Scale (EWS) Company, headquartered in Seymour, Connecticut.

Walter is 91 years young. As far as I know, he is the senior-most active CEO in the scale industry, as well as in America. His life story is both legendary and ordinary, but uniquely American ...

1. Childhood
Walter was born in Garfield, New Jersey, in 1922, as the third and youngest son to immigrant parents. Walter's father emigrated from Germany to the U.S. in 1910, seeking and hoping to make a better life for his wife and his future children.

Garfield was a small mill town and most of the citizens came from Europe - Irish, French, Germans, Italians and others. They came by the thousands to the U.S., a place known as the "Land of Opportunity".

Family life for Walter was joyful. Loving and hardworking parents made life a wonderful experience, although in retrospect, he realized his family had been poor. Walter and his brothers grew up with a deep and abiding love of, and belief in, God.

Walter enjoyed sports, and played football for Garfield High School, achieving All-State Honors. A string of 22 victories without a defeat earned Garfield High School the honor of playing Miami High School for the U.S. National High School Championship, referred to as "an Infantile Paralysis Bowl" in honor of President Franklin D. Roosevelt! The game was played at today's Orange Bowl site. Garfield was victorious and named the U.S. National High School Football Champions!

An omen of things to come!

2. Early adulthood

After high school, Walter's parents insisted on further education. In 1940, Walter attended Newark College of Engineering, seeking a degree in Mechanical Engineering.

The world was in turmoil and World War II was in full fury. Walter believed it was time to volunteer: he joined the Army Air Corp. and studied to become an Air Corp Meteorologist with the rank of 1st Lieutenant. He served for three years with duty in North Africa and Europe.

3. Climbing the corporate ladder

After his return from the war, Walter completed his mechanical engineering education, graduating in 1948. His first job was with the Richardson Scale Company, a manufacturer of automatic industrial scales and batching systems. He specialized in mechanical and electrical scale system design and then he was asked to move into sales engineering, becoming Vice President of Sales & Marketing.

Walter gives full credit to Mr. Ingram Richardson, President of Richardson Scale Company, for his success in the company. Mr. Richardson saw some potential in Sales and Marketing for Walter that he himself did not see.

In the early 1960s, Richardson Scale was acquired by the Robert Morse Corporation, a Canadian firm that owned Howe Scale Company and other scale and non-scale organizations. Walter served as Vice President of Sales & Marketing for the combined Howe Richardson Scale Company.

These were days of active mergers and acquisitions. The entire Robert Morse Corporation was sold to the large and powerful Aerojet Corporation, a division of the General Tire and Rubber Corporation.

Walter rose to become the President and CEO of the Howe Richardson Scale Company. However, it became apparent that change was the order of the day, and it was time to run his own show, completely.

4. Striking out

Walter looked for new opportunities. Finally, he and a few associates purchased the A.H. Emery Corporation, a small specialty manufacturer of hydraulic load cell weigh systems with annual sales of less than one million dollars.

In 1974, The A.H. Emery Company acquired a small manufacturer of mechanical truck and wagon scales with the great name of the Winslow Government Standard Scale Works located in Terre Haute, Indiana. The A.H. Emery and Winslow Scale were combined to form what is currently the Emery Winslow Scale (EWS) Company.

In 2003, EWS acquired the Pennsylvania Scale Company located in Lancaster, PA, a manufacturer of electronic counting, bench, floor, postal and baggage scales.

Today, EWS manufactures, exclusively in the USA, a wide variety of scale products, including a line of Hydrostatic load cells whose capacity ranges from 100 lb. to 1,000,000 Ib. EWS also manufactured the largest capacity load cell ever made: 12,000,000 Ib. It was designed and built for the National Bureau of Standards.

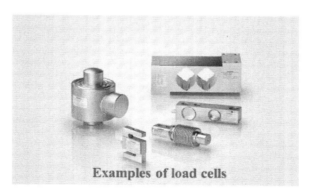

Examples of load cells

Currently, the EWS product line includes truck and track scales, tank and hopper scales, floor and bench scales, tension measurement systems, process control weighing systems, and a variety of custom designed weigh systems. The picture below shows a killer whale sliding up on a 9 by 15 foot platform scale designed to hold up to 40,000 pounds.

Throughout his life in business, Walter experienced many events, some wonderful and some tragic and sad, including numerous recessions, limited cash flow, bank loan refusals, and constantly pledging all his possessions.

In summary, Walter states EWS has been blessed. On top of paying its fair shares of taxes, EWS has never missed a single payroll to its employees!

EWS currently has approximately 70 employees and manufactures all its products in the USA, with facilities in Seymour (Connecticut), Lancaster (Pennsylvania), and Terre Haute (Indiana).

5. Balance in life

Despite the busy life in business, Walter keeps himself balanced in many ways. For example, he served the Lord as a Pastor and Rector of a church and served in a pastoral capacity for over 35 years.

Walter credits many others for helping and advising him along the way. While he agreed to have me write about him for my series of "America: A Nation of Self-Made Men (and Women)", Walter firmly states that a self-made man does not describe his long industrial career. Rather, he had help along the way from many wonderful and caring people, such as Mr. Richardson in Walter's early career.

6. Closing

EWS is a privately held family company and succession is an on-going concern. Walter has three sons active in the business, each with important company responsibility of sales, finance, and manufacturing.

Walter states that his company's mission has always been to manufacture magnificent highly reliable industrial weighing systems that bring total satisfaction to their customers.

Walter expects his company to continue his legacy way beyond him …

Chapter 35: Jon Stimpson: A Self-Made Man!

Jon Stimpson is the owner and president of National Scale Technology, based in Huntsville, Alabama.

Experience has made Jon very philosophical about life. Here is one of his guiding principles: Life is filled with opportunity and adversity. Every one experiences both. The ones who succeed are the ones who best handle the adversities. Some even turn them into opportunities ...

Jon was born in Hartford, Connecticut in 1951. After university, he worked for an insurance company, because there were no jobs available in his chosen field: engineering. Several years later, one "real" job became available and his career finally began.

It quickly became apparent to him that sales engineering, not just engineering, would be the most lucrative and offered the best advancement opportunities. So he specifically aimed his efforts in that direction. However, 10 years later, he found himself unemployed, with a young family. Major adversity!

An employment agency presented an opportunity in sales engineering for a company that made "string gage" load cells, a key component in electronic scales. Jon was not even conversant enough with them to tell him they were strain gage, not string gage. But he eventually accepted the job anyway, out of the family need.

It turned out to be a very good fit for him, definitely an opportunity from the adversity he was facing at that time. He would probably still be with that company today, but thanks to corporate mergers and downsizing, he was left unemployed again after 10 years there. More adversity!

He did manage to have several job offers, but none aligned well enough with his needs. So he decided to take the plunge and start his own company, founding Measurement Specialists in 1990.

Fortunately, he had enough experience and exposure at his previous employer to continue designing and selling load cells and systems. He started as a distributor, using his life savings to buy and stock as many load cells as possible. For two years, he did not pay himself a single cent!

The early success allowed the time necessary to design-in products with new customers, fueling future growth. Also it quickly became apparent to him that there were load cell needs not met by his suppliers. As a result, other manufacturers' products were added to the product line. One of those added was National Scale and Repair in Huntsville, Alabama.

Being a distributor, even a value-added one, is risky. It was becoming apparent the upstart internet was changing the way everyone did business. To assure future success, Measurement Specialists needed to control at least some of the manufacturing of the products sold. Ironically, Jon's former employer was available for sale and Measurement Specialists became a potential buyer. However, at that point, his former employer was not profitable enough to justify the cost.

Attention was turned to National Scale. They were a small, profitable manufacturer whose biggest distinction was that they repaired virtually any other manufacturers' load cells, or made copies of them. An agreement was reached and Measurement Specialists purchased National Scale and Repair.

After overcoming many problems typical with any acquisition within the first few years, Jon replaced the management team and renamed the company "National Scale Technology" (or NST) to reflect the company's ability to design and build new products. Since then, NST has been hugely successful. For example, NST has been part of the "Return to Flight" program for the U.S. Space Shuttle, and is one of a selected few authorized manufacturers to build load cells for lifting the caps off nuclear reactors. Many customers come to NST to solve seemingly unsolvable force measurement/weighing problems. NST has several patents for its unique work, including the only patented on-board weighing system for railroad cars.

Success from adversities turned into opportunities!

NST currently has about 30 employees. It is one of the few companies still making load cells in the U.S.!

Succession in a closely held company is always a concern of the owner. It is Jon's intent to pass along his company to his two daughters. Both of them have been with the company for over 15 years. One of them has been managing operations while the other has been managing sales.

All in the family!

Chapter 36: Fred Herrmann: A Self-Made Man!

Fred Herrmann is the owner and president of INScale (or Indiana Scale Company) based in Terra Haute, Indiana.

Fred was born in the Bronx, New York, in 1941. After graduating from high school, he enlisted in the Air Force. Shortly after discharging from the Air Force in 1963, he joined the scale industry.

He worked for several scale companies until 1990, when he finally founded his own company INScale. It was out of a very difficult situation, both professionally and personally. However, in hindsight, he was glad for the situation, because that allowed him to be his own boss, finally!

INScale specializes in making floor scales. Fred holds several patents on floor scales, and is known as the "floor scale man" in the scale industry. The image below shows an example floor scale.

Like many scale companies, INScale has had its own share of ups and downs over the past two decades. Today, Fred is proud to say that INScale is the only scale company in the U.S. that was founded exclusively to make floor scales and it is still in business, at the same location (Terre Haute, IN) producing the same product!

INScale currently has 12 employees. It is more profitable than its heydays, when it employed more than 20 people. What's the trick? Quick adaptation and constant improvement! Here are three business tips Fred wants to share with the world:
1) Treat your employees very well.
2) Don't pillage your business.
3) Be honest.

Married to the same woman since 1959 and semi-retired now, Fred is enjoying his life to the fullest extent, after surviving a heart attack and colon cancer in 2012.

Finally, on the notion of "there is no success without succession", Fred has this to say: "I have eight children and I wish they will all become self-made men (and women) like me!"

Chapter 37: Pin Ni: "His Own Warren Buffett"

Google "Saving America, Chinese Style" and see what happens ... Aside from a list of news stories about my book (Saving America, Chinese Style), you will see this article: Wanxiang America's Pin Ni is snapping up factories, saving jobs ... Read the article to see how much you are impressed by this guy named Pin Ni.

Pin and I go way back to China, as both of us graduated from Zhejiang University. Although he was a few years junior, I knew him well, as he was a classmate of my younger brother's - Pin was said to be a genius, truly ...

In 1994, Pin showed up in Chicago, trying to start his own company. By then, I was already a well-polished corporate dude, properly dressed and well versed in English. In contrast, he was a "diamond in the rough". He was rough because his English was very broken and he was just too Chinese by any standard. But he was a diamond because there was never any doubt in my mind that he would be successful, given his background and his ability. The only question was how soon and how big ...

Well, less than twenty years later, he has succeeded beyond the wildest dream of any human being! Three points:
1) He has proven to be one of the most successful Chinese businessmen in America!
2) His company, Wanxiang America, has proven to be one of the most successful Chinese companies in America, with revenues from $0 in 1994 to $2B in 2012!
3) He has been called "his own Warren Buffett".

Wanxiang America, Elgin, IL, USA

Pin, I am very proud of you both as a friend and as a business partner!

What's your take-away from here? Saving America, Chinese Style is not just a "nice theory" in a nice book! It's already happening, bottom-up. What we need now is some top-down actions, initiated by the next President of the United States!

Part 9: America: Let's Have Some Fun!

Chapter 38: Ice Hockey: Let's Get Rid of the Goalie!
Chapter 39: Obese: to Be or Not to Be (II)?

Chapter 38: Ice Hockey: Get Rid of the Goalie!
(Initially published at GEI on 5/30/2013)

The NBA season ended prematurely for the Chicago Bulls this year. But who cares – Our focus has been on the Blackhawks anyway. You see, in this great sports city of Chicago, anything short of a championship is considered a failure. So the money has been on ice hockey this year ...

Americans are sports fanatics. We are crazy about many sports: basketball, football, baseball, and you name it ... But if you are really into sports, you should like ice hockey more than any other sports, for three main reasons, at least:
1) It's much faster, as an NHL player can reach a maximum speed of 30 miles/hour.
2) It's much more confrontational, as it's often highlighted in the news with fist fights.
3) It's much more physical, as many players have missing teeth.

In short, ice hockey is a real sport!

Why, then, isn't ice hockey more popular in the U.S. than basketball or football? Well, aside from the fact that ice hockey is just too popular in Canada, as we Americans do not like to be second in anything, the game itself is to blame! Specifically, it's the goalie, stupid!

With the goalie, ice hockey is just like soccer, a game of futility, mostly! See, we Americans are very result-oriented: you either score or you don't – There is nothing in between! Additionally, we enjoy instant gratification and constant highlights more than other people.

Without the goalie, ice hockey could be as high scoring as basketball, which would make LeBron James look only too slow and only too human.

Attention NHL: to gain more fans, change the rules and enliven the game by getting rid of the goalie! This is a serious proposal. Once you do that, other sports (e.g. Lacrosse and Water Polo) will follow!

Go Blackhawks! Bring back the Stanley Cup again, this year!

The Blackhawks did – They won the Stanley Cup in 2013!

Now, repeat in 2014 and make a proud fan like me more proud!

Chapter 39: Obese: to Be or Not to Be (II)?
(Initially published at GEI on 8/1/2013)

A little more than one year ago (on June 15, 2012), I published this article: Obese: to Be or Not to Be. Two big things have happened since then:
1) The article has been a major hit, with almost 5,000 page views, so far.
2) American Medical Association Classifies Obesity as a Disease.

So it's time for me to re-visit the subject with additional insights ...

A Chinese college classmate of mine spent two months touring around the U.S. in 2012. It was her first time in the U.S. and she was deeply impressed. Among many things, America's natural beauty and the richness in natural resources were most impressive to her.

However, she also remarked negatively about America. Here is a conversation we had:

Friend: The U.S. is too rich in natural resources for China to compete against.
Frank: Yes, that's true.
Friend: But I find some hope for China.
Frank: Oh, what is it?
Friend: There are too many fat people in America.
Frank: Why is that any hope for China?
Friend: Being fat means a lack of self-control. When you have so many fat people, it reflects the culture and the nation that way: a lack of self-control.

What an astute and insightful observation! As a Chinese-American, I can easily see her viewpoint ...

Here is a highlight from a recent U.N. report on obesity:

Country	Prevalence of obesity among adults (2008)
China	5.6%
The U.S.	31.8%
Japan	4.5%
Mexico	32.8%

No wonder my Chinese friend felt "Americans are fat": 5.6% vs. 31.8%!

But does the fact that "Americans are fat" rise up as the biggest factor to determine the winner of the head-on competition between the U.S. and China, as my Chinese friend thought? Let's reason ...

To me, here are three main reasons Americans are so much fatter than the Chinese:
1) Life style: Obesity is a life style - eating too much; exercising too little! Unfortunately, many Americans are looking for excuses, blaming anything and everything but themselves!
2) Culture: Americans embrace freedom, including the freedom to be fat, while the Chinese emphasize greater self-control, from Confucius of more than 2,500 years ago to today. Many differences between the two cultures are reflected in the subject of obesity, from the reality to the attitude toward it. The single Chinese character shown below is perhaps the most important character in the Chinese language to convey the Chinese philosophy and wisdom: it literally and pictorially means to put up with everything, even if it means to have a knife stabbed at your heart, in order to be successful. The Chinese credo is pretty tough, huh?

3) Prosperity: America has simply been far more prosperous than China! Yes, the Chinese are becoming fatter and fatter, thanks to their newfound prosperity and the relentless invasion of western food (and culture) ...

Bottom line: the Chinese will be fatter as they become more prosperous, but they will never catch up with Americans in obesity for many reasons, not the least of which is the difference in culture!

Obesity is very bad – It's the root cause for many health problems! When you have 1/3 of the adult population obese as in the U.S. today, it's clearly a national problem. It's quite possible that this problem can be so bad that the race for superiority between the U.S. and China will come down to this: who can avoid obesity better?

My fellow Americans, here is a clear choice for our weight: more self-control or more government intervention? I like the former, but we seem to be heading in the direction of the latter ...

Oh, for those Americans who blame everybody but themselves, here is some good news from the U.N. report: Although the U.S. is still the most obese nation among the "countries in developed regions", our neighbor Mexico is now one full percentage point ahead of us (32.8% vs. 31.8%)!

Now, for those who blame prosperity for obesity, look at Japan: 4.5% vs. America's 31.8%!

Needless to say, obesity is such a complex subject that it's simply impossible to cover it in a short article like this - I have just given you another perspective - at least consider it!

Want to read more? Here are three articles I read before writing this article:
1) Chris Christie Had Secret Weight-Loss Surgery.
2) Is obesity a disease? Experts sound off.
3) I'm fat, and it's my fault – other reactions calling to obesity a disease.

Oh, in case you are concerned about the PC (political correctness) of this article, I am not – I hate PC! For more, read Chapter 27 ("America: What The Heck Is All This Political Correctness?").

Part 10: Going beyond America

Chapter 40: Lee Kuan Yew
Chapter 41: Li Dexin and Lee Kuan Yew
Chapter 42: 'Everything You Think You Know about China is Wrong,' Really?
Chapter 43: Reading "The Communist Manifesto"

Chapter 40: Lee Kuan Yew
(Initially published at GEI on 3/7/2013)

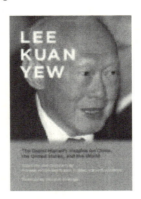

As part of the research for my book (Saving America, Chinese Style), I searched "China" for all the books about China at Amazon.com. The book about Lee Kuan Yew (shown above) stood out. I bought the book, read it, and reached a simple conclusion that has been in my mind for quite some time: Lee Kuan Yew is like Sarah Palin in several ways! I posted my opinion as a "Customer Review" at Amazon.com, but drew some harsh criticism. After responding briefly in the form of comments, I decided to write and publish this article to put my whole argument in perspective.

1. Who is Lee Kuan Yew?
According to Wikipedia,

> **Lee Kuan Yew** (born **Harry Lee Kuan Yew**, 16 September 1923[2]), GCMG, CH, is a Singaporean politician.[3][4][5][6] Often referred to by the initials **LKY**, he was the first Prime Minister of the Republic of Singapore, governing for three decades. He is also widely recognized as the founding father of modern Singapore.

As the co-founder and first General Secretary of the People's Action Party (PAP), he led the party to eight victories from 1959 to 1990, and oversaw the separation of Singapore from Malaysia in 1965 and its subsequent transformation from a relatively underdeveloped colonial outpost with no natural resources into a "First World" Asian Tiger. He is one of the most influential political figures in Asia.[7]

2. Lee is an accomplished man!

Lee is the founding father of modern Singapore. Today, Singapore is a world leader in several categories, such as the standard of living and education, thanks, almost entirely, to his strong and exceptional leadership!

3. Lee was a world statesman!

Lee was a world statesman [especially on China] for two main reasons:

1) His accomplishments in Singapore.
2) The China vacuum: The lack of an alternative Chinese face on the world stage from 1960 to 1990, during which China screwed itself up badly! Lee is a Chinese (by heritage), and he thinks and speaks like a Chinese, which is far more significant than reason #1!

4. Lee has been overhyped!

In analogy, Lee is like Sarah Palin in several ways as follows:

1) He managed a small economy. For example, Singapore is 1/5 in population and geography as compared with Shanghai! Palin's Alaska to the U.S. is more than 20% of Shanghai to China!
2) He rose to the occasion because of the "China vacuum". Palin rose to the occasion because John

McCain was so hopeless and desperate that he had nothing to lose. So he picked Palin as his running mate in 2008 as a shock therapy. Palin would otherwise have had no chance at all to possibly be just one heartbeat away from the American Presidency! Hey, do not underestimate Palin: She actually had more executive experience than Barack Obama by 2008!

3) Both of them should be irrelevant now, because the circumstances for their rises have fundamentally changed.

5. Lee should be irrelevant now

Lee should be irrelevant as a world statesman by now for one simple reason: China is back, and there are some "real" Chinese out there who think, write, and speak far better than Lee! Any doubt? Just compare this book with mine (Saving America, Chinese Style)!

While Lee's understanding of China is largely correct, his understanding of the West and democracy is so yesterday that he should perhaps immediately retire himself to seclusion half way through my book!

Oh, in case you are unaware, Singapore has never been a true democracy *per se* for even a single day! Lee ruled like a king for 30 years, and his son is the Prime Minister now! Despite the fact that more than 70% of the population in Singapore are Chinese descents who speak Chinese, the government "worked over the past 40 years to establish English as our first language, and Chinese as the second" (page 203 of 1613, Kindle Edition) – What an accomplishment! It may well change itself back in 20 years though …

6. The China vacuum

I have long maintained that the biggest regional losers as a result of China's rise are the following:
1) Country: Hong Kong! It is no longer the financial center of Asia! Shanghai is, instead!
2) Individual: Lee Kuan Yew! He has been increasingly marginalized as a statesman! Watch out: there will be a lot more "real" Chinese coming out as statesmen in the coming years!

So be very careful in your response to a "loser"! Two examples:
1) Hong Kong: The people of Hong Kong suddenly started demanding democracy, which they never had under the British rule of 100 years, right before 1997, when China was about to take over!
2) Lee Kuan Yew: His continued advocacy for a stronger U.S. presence in East Asia is not only self-serving, but also U.S.-destroying! We, the U.S., have been saving the world while bankrupting ourselves at home! Additionally, read this: Be wary of rising China, says Lee Kuan Yew. What a sore "loser"!

7. Bottom line

Lee managed a small country/city (about 3M people by the time Lee retired) with excellence - That was it!
1) Economically, both Taiwan and South Korea did equally well, if not better. Remember: size matters! Building a perfect house on a street corner is very different from building the Palace of Versailles!
2) Politically, Lee ruled like a king for 30 years. He did advocate democracy, but that was "for everybody but us, because we are too small to afford any mess up."

8. Closing

Lee Kuan Yew is an accomplished man! The folks in Singapore should remember him well into the future. But that's it, no matter how much hype is out there to project him as a world leader beyond Singapore. He was not, is not, will never be!

Lee was a *de facto* king after all, which is fundamentally against the western values! Therefore, the western elites should stop worshiping him like the North Koreans do with the Kims!

We live in a complex world, with winners and losers in every area. What does it take to be a winner in what you do? Among many things, a shaper vision of the future! Perpetuation of the past must be tempered with a correct view of the future. Read my book (Saving America, Chinese Style), and you will be much better prepared, guaranteed!

Chapter 41: Li Dexin and Lee Kuan Yew
(Initially published at GEI on 4/4/2013)

The image above shows Li Dexin, my late father, and Lee Kuan Yew, the former Prime Minister of Singapore. Are they similar? Yes, in some ways - Hear me out …

By the time this piece is published, I'll be in China. April 4th (or 5th, depending on the Chinese calendar) is Qingming Festival in China. It is a national holiday to remember the departed, especially your relatives, by visiting their final resting places. In my case, it means to commemorate my father by visiting his tomb, as shown below (the picture was taken on February 9, 2013, the eve of the Chinese New Year).

Since so many people will be doing the same on this day, all cemeteries will be very crowded. "Tradition" dictates you must visit on this day of Qingming Festival the first three years. After that, it's not necessary to visit on this day and add to the crowds. Instead, any day around that time is fine.

All this is new to me for two main reasons:
1) My father's death was the first death of a family member I have ever experienced.
2) I remember Qingming Festival, but have no memory of such a tradition with so much delicacy, as I left China in 1982. It turned out that it was a long-standing tradition, but Mao had destroyed it under his rule (1949-1976). Many similarly eradicated traditions have been restored since Mao's death in 1976.

I already wrote about my father upon his death almost one year ago (My Father Li Dexin). Allow me to remember him this time by comparing him with Lee Kuan Yew, about whom I just wrote (Chapter 40: "Lee Kuan Yew") too. The two main reasons for this comparison:
1) My father admired Lee very much. He had nothing but praise for Lee.
2) Having visited China twice a year over the past eight years, I was able to spend some quality time with my father (and mother). To strike a good conversation and to please him over the last two years, I often compared him with Lee. He liked it and laughed loudly ...

It's time to make a public comparison!

1. Li and Lee are alike

1) They were born four months apart. Li was born in January 1924, while Lee was born in September 1923.
2) Li and Lee both loved/love their own country, which is China and Singapore, respectively.
3) Li and Lee both were/are politicians, with outstanding achievements.

2. Li and Lee are different

1) Li was a real Chinese, born in China and dying there too. Lee is of Chinese descent, having spent his entire life outside China.
2) Li was a communist, although by name only later in life. Lee was, may still be, a strong anti-communist.
3) Li is not internationally known, but Lee is.

3. Li had greater success than Lee

1) Li turned around two "districts" in China: Jinhua and Hangzhou; each is far larger than Singapore. For example, Hangzhou (district) has at least twice more the population and geography than are found in Singapore! As for the importance of the city of Hangzhou, here is a tip: when President Nixon visited China in 1972, he visited three cities: Beijing, Hangzhou, and Shanghai, in that order!
2) Li helped develop and served in a political system with term-limits, while Lee ruled like a king for 30 years. Note that term-limits may be bad for individuals, but it's almost always good for the long-haul, system-wise. For more, read: Towards An Ideal Form of Government.
3) None of Li's children entered politics – They have all become self-made men (and a woman)! Lee's

son is now the Prime Minister in Singapore - nepotism, perhaps?

Hangzhou, China

4. Lee did better than Li
1) Singapore is a world-class city/country today, coming from nowhere in 1959, when Lee took over. Hangzhou is far away from that status.
2) Lee enjoys huge popularity worldwide, while Li remains totally unknown outside of China (More on Li Dexin).
3) Lee's son is now the Prime Minister in Singapore, while none of Li's children is even in politics at all.

5. My father and me
Here is an old saying: "when people age, they tend to revert to their childhood." I noticed that in my father! For example, about a year before he passed away, he murmured, out of the clear blue, to my sister: "I think my mom should be very proud of me, right?"

What was he thinking as an 87-year-old man then? He was reflecting upon his entire life, starting from the expectations of his parents!

Oh, my God, that's me, in some 35 years. So let me best prepare myself for that …

Here is a conversation he and I had in November 2011:

Son: "What was your biggest achievement?"
Dad: "Turning around Hangzhou, obviously."
Son: "Will that be good enough for you to be in (Chinese) history?"
Dad: "No! How many people can really make history?"
Son: "I think I can."
Dad: "How?"
Son: "With my pen, writing about politics."
Dad: "Oh, yeah, good luck!"

Note the sarcasm? Behind that was a high expectation, to me, at least! So for me, writing about politics is not just a hobby, but a way to please my father! What's better? I think I am part way there already! Any doubt? Compare the two books shown below, and you will see the differences between Lee Kuan Yew and me: my view of China, the U.S., and democracy is simply far superior to Lee's. You be the judge!

6. Closing

Both Li Dexin and Lee Kuan Yew had substantial lifetime achievements! They both rose to the occasion, and left (or will leave) the world a better place than they found. What about the rest of us? Shouldn't we all strive for the same, at least?

Now, to my fellow Americans: if you are reasonably astute, you should know America is deeply in trouble. If you are minimally patriotic, you should read my book (Saving America, Chinese Style), in which I have provided the most accurate diagnosis for America, as well as the best solution. You be the judge!

As for me personally, I hope to have better things to report to my father in April 2014 ... Meanwhile, rest in peace, Dad ...

Chapter 42: 'Everything You Think You Know about China is Wrong,' Really?
(Initially published at GEI on 4/11/2013)

Hello from China! Again, it's time for me to write about China to my fellow Americans, from China!

Have you seen this article: "Everything You Think You Know About China Is Wrong"? I did, quite a few months ago.

What a sensational title! But the content is so yesterday that I commented with two simple questions:
1) How often does the author visit China?
2) When was he in China last time?

To my surprise, Prof. Minxin Pei replied as follows:
1) "I visited China, on average, 3-5 times a year for the past 13 years."
2) "I was in China at the end of April 2012."

So he knows China, both yesterday and today, just as well as I do! Why, then, are we totally opposite in our views of China, today and tomorrow? More importantly, who is right?

Prof. Pei (resume) and I (My American Dream Has Come True) are similar in two ways:

1) Both of us earned an under-graduate degree in China in 1982. Mine is in engineering, while his in liberal arts.
2) Both of us have lived more time outside China than inside. Additionally, I think my two graduate degrees from the University of Tokyo (a.k.a. "The Harvard of Japan") and Vanderbilt (a.k.a. "The Harvard of the South") compare well to his Ph.D. degree from Harvard (a.k.a. "The Vanderbilt of the North").

We are different in two critical ways:
1) He is an academic scholar (i.e. a liberal most likely), while I am a self-made businessman (i.e. a conservative most likely). He writes for a living, for which popularity matters, while I write for fun, for which popularity is less important.
2) He has been writing about China throughout his career, while I started just a few years ago, which is to my advantage: he has to stick to the same line for continuity, while I had the luxury of a fresh look, being much older and wiser at the start.

As a matter of fact, I was following the same line of thinking 15 years ago as Prof. Pei is today. I could even have written a similar article like his then, had I not been too busy with my career in IT (Information Technology). Fortunately, I did not do that, or I would be totally embarrassed today. Unfortunately and understandably, Prof. Pei appears to have been writing along the same line over the past two decades, without fundamental changes, despite the fact that China has fundamentally changed. For example, China's GDP was about $445B in 1990, but more than $7T in 2011!

The good news is that each of us has our own list of publications for you to judge. The bad news is that his view is more popular than mine in America, which could put the U.S.-China relations in serious jeopardy!

I have published a lot about China, with my book Saving America, Chinese Style summarizing them all.

Here are my three simple messages to my fellow Americans:
1) China is a competitor, not an enemy. Everything China does is for her own interest, which, unfortunately, happens to be unseating the U.S. as #1 in economy. Worse yet for the U.S., this competitor has been getting better only, while we are not getting better fast enough, if at all.
2) The U.S. can learn a lot from China, and *vice versa*, from a big subject like free trade to a vast subject like democracy (Towards An Ideal Form of Government).
3) Here is a quote: *"America will never be destroyed from the outside. If we falter and lose our freedoms, it will be because we destroyed ourselves."* Who said it? **Abraham Lincoln**!

Most importantly, I believe I have the most accurate diagnosis for America, as well as the best solution. Yes, I linked them both directly to China (Saving America, Chinese Style)!

In the U.S., there is a lot of misinformation about China for two main reasons:
1) Brainwashing.
2) Some people, including Prof. Pei perhaps, are just trying to make a living, as life can be tough for the folks with degrees in liberal arts. For example,

there are so many scholars whose life has been banked on democracy that any deviation from that could put their livelihood in jeopardy. How can you possibly expect them to think outside of the box for a massive subject like "democracy, as we practice it today, does not work"? It would be totally suicidal for them, career-wise!

Bottom line:
1) You must recognize the real experts and listen to them!
2) Everything possible must be done to avoid conflicts between the U.S. and China, the two largest economies on earth today! The best way to do that is via improved understanding and communication.

Speaking of understanding and communication, here is my simple explanation of the two most important phenomena in the world today:
1) What's the reason behind China's rise? Capitalism!
2) What's the reason behind America's decline? Destructive socialism!

The Chinese should be grateful to President Nixon for opening the door in 1972, so should all Americans - President Nixon proved to be one of the best American Presidents in [recent] history. For more, read Chapter 12 ("Barack Obama vs. Richard Nixon")!

Finally, be very careful about the dissidents, both the dissident people and the dissident views, be they the Chinese dissidents today or the Iraqi dissidents before the Iraq War. They can be very dangerous. We saw it in the case of Iraq (Yes, the Iraqi dissidents encouraged the

U.S. to launch the Iraq War) and let's hope we will not see it in the case of China.

Both the U.S. and China should, and can, learn a lot from each other!

Peace and prosperity, not war and debt!

Chapter 43: Reading "The Communist Manifesto"

I already identified seven similarities between communism and democracy (Chapter 26: "Patriotism: A Seventh Similarity between Communism and Democracy"). In order to best appreciate these similarities, I urge you to scan through The Communist Manifesto. It has only 32 pages and its Kindle edition is free.

The followings are some excerpts from The Communist Manifesto, with my own interpretations.

"The discovery of America, the rounding of the Cape, opened up fresh ground for the rising bourgeoisie."

My interpretation: America is a nation of self-made Men! For more, read Part 8.

"The theory of the Communists may be summed up in the single sentence: Abolition of private property!"

My interpretation: No private property, no prosperity - Been there, done that!

"We Communists have been reproached with the desire of abolishing the right of personally acquired property as the fruit of a man's own labor, which property is alleged to be the groundwork of all personal freedom, activity and independence."

My interpretation: No personal property, no freedom! For more, read Chapter 5 ("The Democratic Party is the Party of New Slavery").

"You are horrified at our intending to do away with private property. But in your existing society, private property is already done with for nine-tenths of the population; its existence for the few is solely due to its non-existence in the hands of those nine-tenths. You reproach us, therefore, with intending to do away with a form of property, the necessary condition for whose existence is the non-existence of any property for the immense majority of society."

My interpretation: 10% vs. 90% or 1% vs. 99%? They both are the same class struggle or class warfare! For more, read Chapter 8 ("Top 10 American Misconceptions about Capitalism").

"We have seen above, that the first step in the revolution by the working class, is to raise the proletariat to the position of ruling as to win the battle of democracy."

My interpretation: Isn't democracy similar to communism?

"The proletariat will use its political supremacy to wrest, by degrees, all capital from the bourgeoisie, to centralize all instruments of production in the hands of

the State, i.e. of the proletariat organized as the ruling class; and to increase the total of production forces as rapidly as possible."

My interpretation: Rob or steal from the rich! If you can't do it by yourself, leverage your government to do it for you! For more, read: Chapter 3 ("Democratic Socialism").

"The communists everywhere support every revolutionary movement against the existing social and political order of things."

My interpretation: Hasn't America been spreading democracy like communism? For more, read Chapter 2 ("Democratic Imperialism").

Bottom line: Does democracy really look like communism to you now?

"Democracy looks more and more like communism, which is opium. Opium makes you feel good in the short term, but is harmful, even fatal, in the long term!"
--- Frank Li

Epilogue

America must be saved! Only the GOP can do it! However, the GOP must save itself first before saving America! 2016 may be the last chance the GOP can possibly save itself and America, because after that it may not matter anymore: America will have so many "takers" (or slaves) that they will choose the President, who will create more of them, until America is destroyed, totally!

As a staunch supporter of Mitt Romney, I was disappointed at the result of the 2012 election. I also feel partially responsible for Romney's loss: my last book (Saving America, Chinese Style) came out too late – It was published after the 2012 election!

With this book out in 2013, I hope to make a big difference in the 2016 presidential election.

In Chapter 1, I listed out four reasons behind the argument that "the GOP is dead" as follows:
1) Democratic imperialism
2) Religion
3) Democratic socialism
4) Ideas (or lack of) for restoring America.

I have subsequently addressed all of them, except for religion. Was this omission an oversight? No, it was not! Religion is too complex for me …

However, here are my three simple messages to the religious right:
1) Do not mix religion with politics! Neither should impose on the other.

2) Stay low during the campaign of the general presidential election, which is mostly about winning the middle 20% of the electorate, anyway. You are in the 40% on the right.
3) Vote!

With that, the strategy for GOP 2016 is complete. All that the GOP needs is a strong presidential candidate who will buy into this strategy.

Will the GOP listen? Let wait and see …

In case you are wondering about my party affiliation, I am an independent with a GOP-leaning voting record.

For a thorough understanding of America, including the best diagnosis for America as well as the best solution, read my last book: Saving America, Chinese Style!

About the Author

Frank (Xiaofeng) Li (厉晓峰) is the Founder and President of W.E.I. (West-East International), a Chicago-based import & export company.

He was born in Hangzhou, China, in 1959, and grew up in the horrible days of the Cultural Revolution. He was a hopeless teenager when China re-opened its universities in 1977, after closing them for more than a decade! He was lucky enough to make into Class 77.

He received his B.E. degree from Zhejiang University (China) in 1982, M.E. from the University of Tokyo in 1985, and Ph.D. from Vanderbilt University in 1988, all in Electrical Engineering. He worked for several companies all over the world until 2005, when he founded his own company W.E.I. Today, W.E.I. is a leader in the scale industry not only in products & services, but also in thought & action.

He started writing about business and politics in 2008. He writes extensively and uniquely about American politics, for which he has been called a "modern-day Thomas Jefferson."

His first book "Saving America, Chinese Style" was published in November 2012. This is his second book.